# ORGANIZATIONAL DEVELOPMENT IN URBAN SCHOOL SYSTEMS

Edited by

## C. Brooklyn Derr

 **SAGE** PUBLICATIONS *Beverly Hills / London* 1974

## PUBLISHER'S NOTE

Most of the material in this publication originally appeared as a special issue of **EDUCATION AND URBAN SOCIETY** (Volume VI, Number 2, February 1974); two of the articles originally appeared in the May 1974 issue of **EDUCATION AND URBAN SOCIETY** (Volume VI, Number 3). The Publisher would like to acknowledge the assistance of the special issue editor, C. Brooklyn Derr, in making this edition possible.

*For information address:*

SAGE PUBLICATIONS, INC.
275 South Beverly Drive
Beverly Hills, California 90212

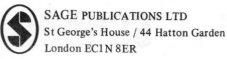

SAGE PUBLICATIONS LTD
St George's House / 44 Hatton Garden
London EC1N 8ER

Printed in the United States of America

International Standard Book Number 0-8039-0439-8

Library of Congress Catalog Card No. 74-78559

FIRST PRINTING (this edition)

# CONTENTS

# A Message from the Editor

**The collection of articles** comprising this special edition are both polemic and empirical. Together, they indicate much about the state of organization development (OD) and its application to education— especially to urban school systems. OD is a relatively new field, about fifteen years old, and has only recently been introduced to educational enterprises. The first book on OD in education was by Schmuck and Miles (1971), and the first field experiments using this technology in schools date back to about 1965.

Each of the authors has his own definition of organization development, but most of them agree that OD is at least three-dimensional. It includes (1) a guiding theory of organizational effectiveness which serves to define the ideal state for which the improvement effort is striving, (2) empirically based assumptions about people (individual and group behavior) in organizational settings and how to create conditions wherein people will perform competently and resourcefully, and (3) a technology for changing complex organizations to help them become more effective (more like the ideal states mentioned above).

Organization development, as an intervention theory and method (see item 3 above), is an iterative process including six sequences of events.

> *(1) Entry.* Establishing the collaborative relationship, ground rules, expectations, and conditions (contract) that will allow for a collaborative effort between parties for organizational improvement.

> *(2) Data Collection.* Collecting valid and useful information that will permit the client system to exercise a free and informed choice about its action alternatives. This often involves a process which prepares the client for joint ownership of the data and for eventual intervention.

*gnosis.* Using applied behavioral science and organizational knowledge, the underlying problems ("blocks") keeping the organization from reaching its objectives and improving its performance are uncovered and made explicit. A technique known as "data feedback" is often employed to validate the analysis and to get the client system to assume ownership for it.

*(4) Intervention.* Using consultant expertise, its own resources, and its own sense of internal commitment (which comes from already deciding to adopt a more "ideal" organization and being in agreement with the diagnosis, thus knowing where the enterprise is in relation to where it wants to go), the client system embarks on a corrective action and improvement program.

*(5) Evaluation.* Assessing the effectiveness of the intervention and modifying ongoing activities to improve effectiveness; doing this in such a way that the emphasis is on promoting learning from experience.

*(6) Withdrawal.* A goal of the consultants is to help the client system as quickly as possible become self-sufficient for its own organization development. The consultant and client will recognize when there is no longer a need for external expertise and the consultant will withdraw from the organization. The OD consultant is ethically bound to withdraw when he is no longer needed or helpful.[1]

The articles included in this special edition follow the sequence of OD events outlined above. Derr and Demb write about the entry phase. They attempt to view an urban school system as a new market for organization development. They suggest that OD specialists should consider knowledge of the culture and context of an organization as essential background for making an entry into such settings. They also stress the utility of performing OD demonstrations (e.g., doing a workshop in problem-solving) and being proactive about contacting client systems as helpful preentry steps.

The Gabarro article is especially useful because of its emphasis on diagnosis. It stresses a contingency theory approach to OD which underscores the importance of appropriately designing corrective actions to fit the situation. The situation is in turn influenced by the external organizational environment. Gabarro also emphasizes structural as well as procedural interventions, whereas, as the reader will note, many of the other manuscripts are more concerned about questions of process. Moreover, Gabarro, Blumberg et al., and Schmuck all report empirical findings which might prove insightful to demonstrate the data collection phase in the OD sequence.

The essay by Blake and Mouton is about intervention. It is important in that it puts OD in broad perspective, as the authors attempt to categorize the possible known action alternatives and apply them to education. The article also presents a conceptual framework, the D/D matrix, which will be useful for readers who wish to understand the various forms of OD that are currently being marketed and discussed. For many, the intervention phase of the OD process is most crucial, for it represents the real potential of the utility of organization development as a technology for organizational change. Blake and Mouton were early pioneers of the whole OD field (see French and Bell, 1973: 23-24).

The articles by Schmuck and Blumberg et al. follow to illustrate possible interventions relevant to inner-city schools. Schmuck's essay outlines some of the major questions involved in trying to intervene in urban school systems. Mainly, how does one involve diverse groups of parents and students in the process? Blumberg and his colleagues give empirical evidence of the utility of OD intervention for a central-city elementary school. These cases describe some of the OD technology in action. These articles may also prove to be most interesting for readers who are new to the field because they are so rich in example and application. In fact, I would suggest that such persons might want to read these three cases first to help illustrate the rest of the material as it appears in sequence.

Finally, Hornstein serves as the critic for this edition. As a professor of social psychology at Teachers College, Columbia, and the Director of the Center for Professional Development of the NTL Institute for Applied Behavioral Science, one of the most active organizations for providing training for OD specialists, he is uniquely qualified to comment.

Two other articles were prepared especially for the original edition of *Education and Urban Society,* but appeared in a later issue of the journal; however, they are included in this *Sage Contemporary Social Science Issues* volume. The article by Joe E. Gentry and J. Foster Watkins, entitled "Organizational Training for Improving Race Relations in Schools," presents findings on the impact of OD training for improving race relations, a topic central to any concern for better urban education. "Developing Leadership Training for Big-City Principals," by Mark R. Shedd, Charles C.D. Hamilton, and Mark T. Munger, describes the limited utility of organization development, and how it was and should be combined with other innovative programs to improve leadership in a big-city school system.

I would like to personally thank the authors for their enthusiastic response to an invitation to join in making this volume possible. They not only agreed to contribute but submitted their articles on schedule, a fact which anyone who has edited a book or journal will immediately appreciate.

*—CBD*

## NOTE

1. Blake and Mouton would differ somewhat from this sequence. They believe that the strategies of organization development are more flexible than this and that the above categories are most congruent with the catalytic approach presented in the D/D matrix in their article written for this issue.

## REFERENCES

FRENCH, W. L. and C. H. BELL, Jr. (1973) Organization Development. Englewood Cliffs, N.J.: Prentice-Hall.

SCHMUCK, R. A. and M. B. MILES [eds.] (1971) Organization Development in Schools. Palo Alto, Calif.: National Press Books.

# ENTRY AND URBAN SCHOOL SYSTEMS
## The Context and Culture of New Markets

C. BROOKLYN DERR
ADA DEMB
Graduate School of Education
Harvard University

**The term "organization development"** describes a process of planned change that is organizationwide and iterative in its examination of problems, design of strategies, and evaluation of outcomes. It is a normative theory which describes effective organization and thus sets certain behavioral and structural goals for the change process. It is also a theory of effective interpersonal relationships which proscribe in large part the consulting relationship (intervention theory) in which OD practitioners act. At present it is one of the most important tools available to organizations interested in developing their potential and effectiveness.

As a profession, OD has grown and developed during the past fifteen years largely within the industrial sector. More recently there have been attempts to expand the use of OD into the public sector, particularly into health care and education, and into the international market. Focusing particularly on attempts to use OD in urban school systems, the authors would like to examine some of the problems associated with introducing this new field to its users, with the hope of furthering understanding on the part of both OD professionals and potential consumers.

## OD THEORY AND A NEW PERSPECTIVE

The phases which an organization development effort takes have been variously described in the literature. Basically, they are: (a) a scouting period during which time the potential consultant becomes acquainted with his potential client in order to determine the probability or feasibility of a matching of needs and expertise; (b) entry—a time when client and consultant explicitly develop, discuss, and contract the situations and conditions of the relationship; (c) a diagnostic phase—in which it is usually primarily the consultant's responsibility to collect data and then in collaboration with the client, identify problems and issues; (d) an action stage—during which time strategies planned as a result of diagnosis are implemented by client and consultant; and (e) an evaluation period—during which time the outcomes of (c) and (d) are reexamined and evaluated for effectiveness in order to plan and diagnose anew for the next iteration (see Kolb and Frohman, 1970).

## ENTRY

Derr (1972), Argyris (1970), and others have identified elsewhere the critical importance of the entry phase mentioned above. In a study of five relationships between urban school systems and universities (Derr and Demb, 1973) the authors have revealed important correlations between those cases where satisfactory collaborative relationships were established and the nature of the entry process which preceded these relationships.

The process of entry, as it is described in the literature, has two major components: a set of preconditions and a sequence of events. The preconditions are:

(1) Relationship-building—the process of building trust, establishing a problem-solving climate, and norms of openness and honesty, and of feeling out issues of power and influence.

(2) Examining prerequisites—exploring explicitly perceptions of client need and consultant helpfulness, client readiness to confront data, and in general, assessing the working relationship.

(3) Contracting—explicitly contracting access to information, collection of data, roles, behavioral norms, ethics, time commitments, and influence patterns.

(4) Points of contact—developing and understanding the actors' links to power, and the nature of the system.

The time frame can be described as six phases of an iterative process:

(1) client senses a problem

(2) client contacts the consultant believing he can help resolve it

(3) initial meetings

(4) preconditions determined, contracting and relationship-building

(5) consultant reorients the client system to other possible problems (the initial problem may be a symptom of an underlying issue)

(6) preconditions redetermined, more contracting

## COLLABORATION

The major generalization which developed from the author's study was that the notion of a collaborative relationship, on which OD consultive theory is based, created a set of expectations about the nature of the relationship whose exploration is not encompassed by entry theory. While entry theory describes a one-way process of a consultant entering an organization, collaboration implies a two-way relationship. That is, viewing the consultant as an expert (with OD technology) about to make his entry into the client organization, little attention (if any) is paid to affecting the consultant organization as a result of the interaction. The client, however, may consider affecting the consultant a critical aspect of the "collaboration."

The notion of collaboration is based on a situation of

mutual need satisfaction and mutual influence. It is an interdependent (power equal) situation, where the interdependence is based on an ability to aid in the solution of a problem. In a collaborative relationship the key variable is the location of problems and agreement upon mechanisms for resolving them. Collaboration implies that there is agreement between two parties, that each has a need, "a problem," and that each is capable of and willing to aid the other in solving his problem.

An example of this generality might be the case of a consulting firm approaching an industrial client. The problem the firm seeks aid in resolving is the earning of profits; the industrial client's problem might be any number of organizational difficulties. Each party is able and willing to solve the other's problem. Each party wields some control over the other. Without the client, the firm loses potential for profit; without the consultant, the industry loses potential aid in solving its organizational dilemma.

In the case just described, each party defines itself as both client and consultant to the other in a set of simultaneous and opposite relationships (see Table 1).

In the Derr and Demb (1973) study, the assumptions of mutual need satisfaction and mutual influence appeared to be the key to understanding those cases where productive collaborative relationships appeared to be blocked. The blocking resulted from a frustrated expectation on the part of either the consultant or client, or their unwillingness to be both a consultant and a client at various moments in the

TABLE 1
CLIENT-CONSULTANT RELATIONSHIP

| Industrial Firm | Consulting Firm | Goal |
|---|---|---|
| (1) Client | Consultant | Resolution of an organizational dilemma |
| (2) Consultant | Client | Financial gain, development of new skills and techniques, public relations |

collaborative effort and on the failure of both partners to engage in open and honest problem-solving behavior in order to achieve a state of interdependence in their relationship.

## THE BROADER PERSPECTIVE

If we expand the notion of collaborative entry from the situation of an individual consultant making contact with a specific client to the situation of a profession making contact with a new category of clients, several major client concerns become more readily apparent. Using "profession" in the sense of the aggregation of individual practitioners and their expertise, we draw an analogy, for a moment, between OD practitioners and the peace corps doctors and engineers of the very early 1960s or the computer experts of the late 1950s.

Both of these sets of professionals appeared untried and unproven to their potential clients, who were, in turn, skeptical and unknowledgeable about the expertise offered. The goals of early interactions between these professionals and the new clients were: (1) to convince the client that the product was useful, (2) to convince the client that the professional possessed that expertise and was not a hack or hoax, and (3) to express a willingness to explore together the problems where the product might be useful and to tailor it so that the consultant could be most useful to the client—either by modifying accessibility or by modifying actual processes. These dialogues, presumably, were specifically aimed at helping the client make the transfer between the applicability and usefulness in other contexts to his own. It is at this point that the analogy is most meaningful to OD professionals and those seeking to expand the usefulness of their product into new areas.

As a profession, organization development is at a point of engaging in these entry conversations with professionals in the fields of education and health care. The process of developing a relationship at an individual level when the larger professional context is yet unproven from the client's perspective is indeed difficult. The entry model that intervention theory provides, can be very helpful in pinpointing areas where an extra effort at communication and flexibility is necessary. Additionally, the sequence of events described by traditional entry theory indicates a need for a new approach which permits the consultant to also sense the problem and contact the client.

While entry theory provides a careful model of the process of responding to client initiatives to establish a collaborative consultative relationship, we feel that it does not approach another critical aspect of this process. The "content" of the entry situation should be as important to specify as the process.

The two aspects of the content that are especially critical at entry are a knowledge of (1) the organizational *context* and (2) the organizational *culture*. The first is composed of the critical factors in the external environment of the enterprise that affects its performance, and the second is comprised of the behavioral norms and value system which permeate the internal environment of the organization. We believe that entry will be more effective and that more satisfactory collaborative relationships will be established if the consultant can demonstrate an understanding of his client's contextual constraints and the culture within which the client must act.

As we suggested, relationship problems at the first stage of entry are most difficult in new markets where OD has not yet been "proven." Urban school systems fall into this category. Shopping for help, big-city school administrators have heard that a new product (OD) exists. They are aware that it has been useful in industry, and has been tried in some suburban school districts with varying degrees of success. They hear advocates from graduate training programs, journal articles, and funding agencies. Yet, urban school administrators are not at all sure that they understand OD or, if they do, that it is a viable alternative for them.

Let us examine several contextual and cultural dimensions of urban school systems to explore their implications for organization development and entry. How much and where might we have to adapt OD to be successful in the city? How can this information be helpful at entry?

## CONTEXT

The *lack of a supportive and compelling environmental force* underlies many of the reasons for the difficulties associated with successful OD entry into urban school systems. The urban school system is not a part of the competitive market which provides much of the stimulation for management-training programs and OD in industry. As it is by law a tax-supported, monopoly enterprise, the school system is not pressed by the market to develop either new products or more effective organization configurations. The system's monopoly status permits the development of greater inertia than in the suburban school systems, which are in competition with one another for wealthy taxpayers (see Derr, 1970; Carlson, 1964). This could mean that people in the school system feel little pressure for systematic and planned improvement programs such as organization development.

In industry, as we have mentioned above, it is the pressure of a competitive environment which stimulates interest in better or more efficient management strategies. In education, the external environment—public and community groups— just now has available to it the information and tools with which to exert this type of creative pressure. For example, voucher systems and alternative school programs begin to create a quasi-competitive market where the monopoly has prevailed. More adequate definitions and performance indicators for a "well-educated student" are now becoming available. In sum, the client is only recently able to evaluate schools critically.

A directly related issue is the *lack of adequate financing* for the city school systems. The city has a poor tax base and, in addition, political pressure for reelection depends on preventing tax increases. State legislators tend to favor the more suburban districts disproportionately. Only recently has the federal government concentrated its funding on the cities, and then very little money has been appropriated for OD kinds of activities. As an "unproven" commodity, organization development is not perceived as so high a priority item than an OD program would be considered for funding at the level and time commitment necessary. In this situation the tradeoff may become OD or books; or OD versus a new school building.

This noncompetitive environment and the lack of adequate financing create a *management-by-crisis orientation* in the urban school district. Derr (1971) has described the vicious circle of crisis orientation that he discovered in one large urban school district. The administration, responding to priority items, reacted first to those crises that could affect its very nature and existence. Some environmental groups sensed that the way to gain attention quickly was to present their demands as crises, so they in turn precipitated events that caused immediate concern and thereby kept the administrators constantly "fighting fires." Further, under these conditions of high stress and anxiety individuals (and systems) tend to become even more aggressive, power-oriented, defensive, and rigid (see Osgood, 1962; Milburn, 1961). Under these circumstances the organization will be highly resistant to a program suggestion which would require the time (for planning) or change (increasing functional flexibility) an OD effort would demand.

A major reason for crisis management is the *vulnerability of the school system vis-à-vis its external environment.* As has been discussed by Bidwell (1965) and Sieber (1968), schools are more vulnerable to these external groups than other types of organizations because schools are client-serving rather than client-gathering. Because they are tax supported they are subject to constant scrutiny by parents and community groups, must be neighborhood relevant, and often double as community center facilities. Because their product is the transformation of human beings, they provoke a high degree of emotional involvement. This is an additional factor which produces the crisis orientation discussed above. For organization development, such vulnerability could mean that people in the school system will perceive fewer proactive alternatives and will be cautious about the public reaction. Additionally, as suggested above, they do not interpret the environmental pressure as a challenge to improve (as do organizations in competition) but, rather, as a need to retrench and defend.

Finally, there is a *lack of required interdependence* in most schools and school systems. Required interdependence is defined as the extent to which persons (or groups) in the enterprise must work together in order to accomplish the goals and tasks. The real points of interdependence in a school or school system occur over summer workshops and in meetings about budget issues, common crises, union activities, and specific committee assignments, of which none may be directly related to teaching. Teaching and the transmittal of knowledge, the major objective of schools, occur in highly autonomous classroom situations.

Indeed, although the situation is beginning to change as there is increased pressure for "open" classrooms and team teaching at this time, the external environment does not necessitate a high degree of interdependence within schools and school systems.

## CULTURE

Examination of another aspect of the lack of required interdependence concerns the *value placed on autonomy* within an urban school. Individual schools operate independently of one another, with the principal as the highest authority. Within schools, teaching is predominantly an individual activity and curriculum specialists and supervisors are careful not to invade the semi-sacred territory of the teacher. They are perceived by all, as consultants, not collaborators.

The need for teacher autonomy is derived, in part, from their semi-professional status. Like nurses and social workers, teachers are at the lower end of the continuum of the professional class. Their knowledge base, training, and ethics are much less developed than doctors or lawyers, for example. Thus, they vigorously seek after professional autonomy, in part as an assurance that they are indeed professionals (for more about the need for teacher autonomy, see Lortie, 1969; Becker, 1964; Dreeben, 1970; Sarason, 1971).

The value placed on autonomy leads to a situation where many collaborative schemes, including organization development, are resisted by those in the organization. It is debatable whether employees in urban systems, and other kinds of districts as well, would opt for collaboration even if the public demanded it.

Further, urban school districts are known for *promoting from within their ranks.* They are often inbred both in terms of administrative positions being staffed by teachers and career veterans, and in terms of positions at the top of the administrative hierarchy being filled by those who have obeyed the informal laws of the organization. Upper management may be composed of people with similar experiences and points of view. Those who are aspiring to be leaders may have more appreciation for experience and conformity than for competence (e.g., new knowledge, advanced training) as requisites for getting ahead. Derr's (1971) research confirms this assertion for one big city system.

Many organizations are inbred and most of them have informal laws (norms) that are followed. Urban school districts, however, tend to be qualitatively more inbred and normative than many other enterprises. As one high-level school board member in one of the nation's largest cities confided to the authors, "What it's all about for the folks who elect us is jobs. We have to either go inside or in the community to make our appointment. We would be crazy to hire some outside expert full-time if we value our own jobs."

The point here is that urban school districts are also important sources of employment for groups in the city who are in power (this idea is also corroborated by some unpublished research done by Cronin, Greenbaum, Derr and Rafel for the Danforth Foundation School Board Studies). Some OD assumptions about acting for effectiveness, making decisions where the information is, letting form (organization structure) depend on function, and hiring external and internal experts that are most helpful may be naive. Big-city school districts are very political organizations. However, the inbred nature of these school districts may be changing as the courts push for more desegregation at all levels of the system (including the adult employment structure) and as HEW Affirmative Action Programs demand equal representation. It is unclear, however, whether these efforts will result in an unfreezing of the school system structure or will simply pass control of the system as it now exists to new hands.

The *extent to which professional schools and educational consultants which train educators are new markets* is the final critical cultural factor. Departments of organizational behavior have been part of business schools for some time now. Not only is OD a new technology in education, but persons who teach it to students and practitioners are still few in number. There are no more than six educational administration departments in the country whose faculty are specialized in the subject matter. Only a few faculties have depth in this area. As a consequence of this and of the promotion practices mentioned above, urban educational administrators in general have not been exposed to organization development. Almost all of the OD work being done in school systems and reported in the literature is being done in suburban school districts. The work in progress in Louisville is a notable exception. Thus, urban educators will have been less exposed to the knowledge and skills of organization development than educators generally.

## SUMMARY

We have identified ten factors which we believe mitigate against the acceptance of an OD effort by a large city school system. A strategy—for an individual or for the profession—which seeks to open and engage urban school systems as a new market, would need to specifically address as many of the factors identified as possible in order to be successful.

Of the ten context-culture factors identified in the article, it would seem that at least six of them involve issues or actors that are beyond the reach of the OD consultant, at least in the short-term view. These factors are either environmental "givens" or represent task requirements which could only be approached through a long-term reorganizational effort. The four other factors, however, seem to lend themselves to either convincing arguments or demonstration (see Table 2).

Clearly the OD profession or professional can do little to affect the environment within which the school system operates; for example, OD consultants can neither encourage a more supportive (competitive) situation, nor can the OD profession provide more funds. At least in the short run, it would be difficult for a consultant to be convincing about the benefits of a more interdependent situation or the costs of placing such a high value on autonomy. These factors can be approached eventually; however, in an entry dialogue we

TABLE 2
**CONTEXT-CULTURE FACTORS OF URBAN SCHOOL SYSTEMS**

| Environmental or Task Constraints | Discussable Factors |
|---|---|
| Lack of supportive and compelling environmental forces | General skepticism or mistrust |
| Lack of adequate financing | Management-by-crisis orientation |
| Lack of required interdependence | Extreme environmental vulnerability |
| High value placed on autonomy | Accessibility of educational consultants |
| Promotion from within | |
| Dearth of professional schools teaching OD | |

feel that few convincing general statements could be made, if any. Finally, the manner in which the school system hires and fires and promotes is clearly a long-range, highly emotional and political issue which few administrators would be willing to discuss in an early conversation.

The following four factors, however, seem to lend themselves to discussion or demonstration at entry. General skepticism of the professional expertise and general lack of trust of an individual are issues which consultants always must address at entry. Relationship-building is a critical aspect of the entry model described earlier. Further, in the case of a new market, the OD profession might have to demonstrate its utility in order to gain trust.

Two organizational difficulties, the management-by-crisis orientation and the environmental vulnerability of school systems, appear to be issues on which OD has particular bearing. OD can provide a means to develop more effective ways of organizing to avoid a crisis orientation systemwide. Additionally, the question of how to deal retroactively with the vulnerability of the system to its constituencies on a day-to-day basis could profitably be addressed. OD skills and analytic approaches could be very helpful to those individuals who must deal with the environment.

Finally, although the consultant can do little about increasing the numbers of professional schools presently teaching OD techniques, he can affect the general accessibility of existing education consultants.

## STRATEGIES

There are, broadly speaking, two categories of entry strategies available to the consultant: written and behavioral. Written material—journal articles, books, and publicity from local workshops—can be made more accessible to a potential client, as can case studies or reference letters from other clients. The basic inadequacy of these strategies is that they provide the client only with vicarious information about a process which is highly interactive and experiential. They provide only descriptive material about a process which is highly dependent on the quality of the relationship established between the client and the consultant as persons.

The behavioral strategy is somewhat described by the model presented earlier. Its major components (objectives) are relationship-building, examining prerequisites, contracting, and examining points of contact. A successful behavioral strategy, therefore, must not only address the system factors outlined above, but must also meet these behavioral objectives.

It is at this point that the importance of organizational training (OT) should be emphasized. OT, as compared to organization development, is short-term OD intervention training designed to help solve immediate organizational problems. OT does not stress total system improvement or system culture change, as does OD; yet, organizational training is used as one of the major methods to facilitate organization development. OT is sometimes subsumed under the action phase of the OD process.

Some urban school administrators are now asking OD specialists to provide short-term workshops for them in, for example, problem-solving, goal-setting, communication, and running effective meetings. Or, they are requesting process consultation in conjunction with some other event (e.g., training in how to use information systems). It is possible to argue that one should refuse such opportunities because they are superficial given the extent of services really required for improvement. The system really needs organization development. The analogy may be getting some short-term relief through medication when, in fact, surgery is really needed for health to be restored.

However, if these occasions for short-term training are viewed as opportunities to demonstrate the new OD product and the OD professional to the new consumer, then the importance of OT could be recognized. In a new market, given the experiential nature of the product, this may be a necessary first step, prior to entry, in developing the relationship with the client. As the computer experts, doctors, and engineers had to demonstrate their viability in the 1950s and 1960s, organizational training may be viewed, not as an irresponsible intervention, but a legitimate part of the entry process.

Finally, the consultant and his professional group can affect the availability and accessibility of OD expertise to the client. Traditional OD entry theory and traditional professional ethics consider that client-consultant contact should always be client initiated. As we have seen in the examples from urban education, however, many factors inhibit an administrator's or teacher's propensity to make that move. If OD is to be a useful tool for these organizations and their personnel, it may need to be offered as such by professionals who have the expertise to describe and demonstrate its applicability. This "selling" aspect of OD entry should be considered as an important step in the process.

Using the phases of an organization development effort described in the beginning pages of this article, we can locate the demonstration and selling aspects in the process. This process occurs between the scouting and entry, the two initial phases. Organizational training and other forms of demonstration comprise a crucial preentry step which provides the client with more information about both OD and the consultant on which to base his choice of strategy.

The phases of an OD effort in a new market situation then become:

(a) scouting

(b) selling

(c) demonstration

(d) entry

(e) diagnosis

(f) action

(g) evaluation

Scouting is the initial search and circumstance which brings client and consultant together. Selling and demonstration then help the two parties to interact more effectively in order to better understand OD and to make choices about using it or a particular consultant, important steps in new market situations where the client does not normally possess enough information to make a careful decision. (In fact, demonstration and selling become an important part of scouting in our model.) Following the demonstration, then, consultant and client are ready to negotiate an entry that will help to assure the success of the OD intervention.

The strategy which we offer for the consideration of both OD professional and school system professionals seeks to address both the critical issues outlined in entry theory (presented on pages 10 and 11) and those factors with which school systems must deal on a day-to-day basis. (1) Selling helps the administrator to find professional aid by encouraging consultant-initiated conversations, thereby increasing the availability of that professional aid. (2) A demonstration workshop situation (organizational training) provides the client an opportunity to see the consultant in action and to personally evaluate his potential usefulness for the system (relationship-building). (3) It provides both parties with an opportunity to try out OD technology and explore its usefulness to the particular issues faced by school system personnel (examining preconditions). (4) It provides a more realistic basis for contracting.

We feel, given the constraints urban school personnel face, that a reconsideration of entry theory is necessary. We have sought to provide one alternative strategy which satisfies both client needs and consultant ethics. Other strategies not only exist but are in need of development. The major objective is to provide potential clients with a tangible application of OD technology and theories, so that it can be evaluated for its usefulness in their context.

# REFERENCES

ARGYRIS, C. (1970) Intervention Theory and Method. Reading, Mass.: Addison-Wesley.

BECKER, H. S. (1964) "The teacher in the authority system of the public school," in A. Etzioni (ed.) Complex Organizations: A Sociological Reader. New York: Holt, Rinehart & Winston.

BIDWELL, C. (1965) "The school as a formal organization," in J. G. March (ed.) Handbook of Organizations. Chicago: Rand McNally.

CARLSON, R. O. (1964) "Environmental constraints and organizational consequences: the public school and its clients," in D. E. Griffiths (ed.) Behavioral Science in Educational Administration. Chicago: Univ. of Chicago Press.

DERR, C. B. (1972) "Successful entry as a key to successful organization development in big city school systems," in W. W. Burke and H. A. Hornstein (eds.) The Social Technology of Organization Development. NTL Institute.

––– (1971) "An organizational analysis of the ___ school system." Ph.D. dissertation. Harvard University.

––– (1970) "Organizational development in one large urban school system." Education and Urban Society 2 (August): 403.

––– and A. DEMB (1973) "Building collaborative relationships: a study of university-urban school system interactions." University Council for Educational Administration and the Leadership Training Institute. (unpublished)

DREEBEN, R. (1970) The Nature of Teaching. Glenview, Ill.: Scott Foresman.

ETZIONI, A. [ed.] (1969) The Semi-Professions and Their Organization. New York: Free Press.

––– [ed.] (1964) Complex Organizations: A Sociological Reader. New York: Holt, Rinehart & Winston.

KOLB, D. A. and A. L. FROHMAN (1970) "An organizational development approach to consulting." Sloan Management Rev. 12 (Fall): 51-65.

LORTIE, D. C. (1969) "The balance of control and autonomy in elementary school teaching." in A. Etzioni (ed.) The Semi-Professions and Their Organization. New York: Free Press.

MILBURN, T. W. (1961) "The concept of deterrence: some logical and psychological considerations." J. of Social Issues 17: 3-11.

OSGOOD, C. E. (1962) An Alternative to War or Surrender. Chicago: Univ. of Illinois Press.

SARASON, S. B. (1971) The Culture of the School and the Problem of Change. Boston: Allyn & Bacon.

SIEBER, S. D. (1968) "Organizational influences on innovative roles," in T. L. Eidell and J. M. Kitchell (eds.) Knowledge Production and Utilization in Educational Administration. Eugene: University of Oregon Center for the Advanced Study of Educational Administration.

# DIAGNOSING ORGANIZATION-ENVIRONMENT "FIT"
## Implications for Organization Development

JOHN J. GABARRO
*Graduate School of Business Administration*
*Harvard University*

**A major purpose of organizational development** (OD) is to help organizations, groups, and individuals become more effective in terms of performance, growth, and satisfaction. Until the middle sixties much of the practice and research of OD specialists concentrated on group and intergroup behavior, with secondary attention to task, and tertiary concern for organizational structure and environment (a notable exception is Argyris, 1964). Since then, however, the OD field has broadened its focus to include an emphasis upon organizational structure as it relates to task and environment. This shift has resulted in a more wholistic approach to OD, in which group training methods are complimented and guided by a diagnosis of what tasks an organization must perform to be adaptive to its environment, and what structure facilitates that adaptiveness.

This trend in OD has coincided with (and grown out of) recent work by organization theorists who have focused on task or environment as important variables (e.g., Burns and Stalker, 1961; Woodward, 1965; Thompson, 1967; Lawrence and Lorsch, 1967). The work of these and other theorists has emphasized that there is no one "best" way to design an organization's structure, since appropriate structure is contingent upon variations in both task and environment, as well as the needs of individuals and groups within the organization. This work has resulted in a body of literature which has been referred to as "contingency theory" (Lawrence and Lorsch, 1967). It offers a number of implications for OD in urban school systems. An important one is that if a school system's environment is undergoing major change, it is likely to require alterations in its structure, tasks, and behavior if it is to remain adaptive to that environment.

This article will focus upon the relationship of organization to environment primarily at the systemwide, rather than the schoolhouse, level.

It will be useful to begin by reviewing briefly several dimensions of environment and task that have been identified by contingency theorists as bearing upon effective patterns of organizational design. Then the article will briefly discuss several dimensions of organization that research suggests are characteristic of effective organization regardless of their task or environment. Finally, suggestions will be offered of how a diagnosis of organization-environment "fit" can be conducted as part of an OD effort in an urban school system, and what some implications are for organization design changes and training interventions.

In this discussion, it will be assumed that achieving an organization-environment "fit" is only one component of the OD program's total design.[1] It is likely that most OD programs will have a number of goals in addition to matching an organization to its environment. Other goals might be directed at increasing interpersonal skills of organization members, improving communications, and developing a capacity within the organization to resolve conflict effectively and improve decision-making. It is also assumed that most OD programs will be directed at building an organizational climate of openness and growth. This discussion will assume these other goals as given, and will mainly focus on organization-environment "fit" and its implications for OD interventions. OD intervention will be treated in terms of both training interventions and organizational design interventions.

## DIMENSIONS OF ENVIRONMENT AND TASK

Environment has been defined in a number of ways by organizational theorists (Duncan, 1972). These include the uncertainty of the information which organizational members use in decision-making (Lawrence and Lorsch, 1967), the external organizations and groups with which an organization must transact to survive (Dill, 1958; Evan, 1966; Thompson, 1967), and the totality of physical and social factors used by organization members in taking action regardless of whether these factors are internal or external to the organization (Duncan, 1972). For purposes of this discussion environment is being thought of in terms of an organization's "task domain" which Levine and White (1961) define as the claims which an organization "stakes out for itself" in terms of clients, tasks, services, and important groups, whether inside or outside of the organization. This is similar to Duncan's definition, although less precise. It offers the advantage of being broad enough to include all of the above factors.

This section will describe several dimensions of environment that have implications for organization. It will also discuss interdependence, a dimension of task, which has been found to be important to organizational structure and behavior.

Organizational theorists have studied many dimensions of environment, but three in particular stand out as being especially salient for organizational design: the degree to which an environment is (a) changing, (b) diverse, and (c) uncertain.

## ENVIRONMENTAL CHANGE

The most extensively researched dimension of organizational environment is change—i.e., the extent to which forces in the environment such as client needs and values, competition, technology, and opportunities are in the process of change. A number of empirical studies show that many effective organizations in *stable* environments are characterized by a high degree of formality or structure, concentration of authority at the top, and moderate emphasis on planning. However, these same studies show that effective organizations in *rapidly changing* environments are characterized by less reliance on formal rules, low formality of structure, greater emphasis on planning, more widely dispursed influence, decision-making at lower levels of the organization, and organizational cultures that are "open" and confronting of conflict (Burns and Stalker, 1961; Dill, 1962, 1958; Emery and Trist, 1965; Starbuck, 1965; Thompson, 1967; Lawrence and Lorsch, 1967).

Many of the reasons for these findings seem manifestly apparent. For example, it makes sense that if the nature of the needs and problems facing an organization are in the process of change, that fixed rules and procedures quickly become outdated. Since change often involves the unknown, problem-solving becomes a more appropriate process than the simple hierarchical application of procedures which are based on past history or precedent.

Recent research also suggests that effective organizational adaptation to major environmental change requires differentiation among important groups within an organization (Gabarro, 1973). This differentiation is needed so that some groups in the organization can focus on initiating and planning the responses needed to adapt while other people deal with the ongoing and immediate demands of the environment. Differentiation is used here to mean differences between subunits in the cognitive and emotional orientations of their members. Differences can exist along many orientations. Those researched so far are differences in goal orientation, orientation to change, time orientation, interpersonal style, and formality of structure (Lawrence and Lorsch, 1967; Allen, 1970; Morse, 1970; Gabarro, 1973). This concept of differentiation does not thus refer to what is called "segmentation"—i.e., division of labor or specialization of knowledge (Lawrence and Lorsch, 1967). The need for differentiation has been found to be especially important when an organization's primary subunits are incapable of initiating change because they are overwhelmed with crises of a short-term, coping nature, as is the case in many urban school systems today (Gabarro, 1973).

**ENVIRONMENTAL DIVERSITY**

A second environmental dimension studied by organizational theorists is diversity, e.g., of client groups (in terms of their needs and values), institutions, other focal groups, and relevant technologies which comprise an organization's environment. Considerable research suggests that the more diverse an organization's environment the greater the functional segmentation of subunits that is required (so that different subunits can relate to different parts of the environment), the greater the decentralization of authority that is needed and the greater the importance of subunit autonomy and planning (Dill, 1958; Thompson, 1967; Perrow, 1967; Lorsch and Allen, 1973).

*Diversity, differentiation, and integration.* In a comparative study of organizations in different environments, Lawrence and Lorsch (1967) found that the more diverse an organization's environment, the greater the internal differentiation needed among subunits if the organization as a whole was to meet environmental demands. This differentiation is necessary so that different parts of the organization can develop orientations which are appropriate for the issues posed by the different segments of the environment. Their work also showed that the higher the differentiation among subunits the more difficult it is for them to collaborate, i.e., integrate their efforts. However, they found that high-performing organizations in all environments had attained greater integration among subunits than the low-performing organizations. Their research showed that effective organizations in highly diverse environments were able to attain a high degree of integration despite their high level of differentiation because they were more effective at decision-making and resolving interdepartmental conflicts. Lawrence and Lorsch identified several factors as contributing to an organization's ability to resolve conflict and achieve integration in the face of high internal differentiation. These included: organizational norms which stressed problem-solving and openness; the use of integrating devices to facilitate conflict resolution (such as interdepartmental teams, task forces, integrating roles); and integrators who were characterized by others as possessing high levels of influence and competence.[2]

## ENVIRONMENTAL UNCERTAINTY

A third dimension is the uncertainty characteristic of an environment, i.e., the difficulty which organizational members have in predicting what will happen in the environment, what actions important groups or clients will take, and what actions the organization should take to best meet those needs. This dimension is to a large degree related to change and diversity because rapid change and diversity are themselves sources of uncertainty (Emery and Trist, 1965; Terreberry, 1968; Duncan, 1972). The work done relating uncertainty to organization suggests that the greater the uncertainty in the environment, the more important it is for the organization to have low formality of structure, and that decisions be made at levels of the organization where the relevant information exists (Thompson, 1967; Lawrence and Lorsch, 1967; Perrow, 1967).

For example, a school system may encounter a sudden

increase of uncertainty it its environment when its community changes abruptly in composition such that children bring new needs and problems which the system has not yet learned how to meet. Under these circumstances, it is likely that learning how to meet these needs will require a great deal of problem-solving by system personnel and that old procedures and patterns of organization may need to be changed.

**INTERDEPENDENCE**

So far, three dimesnions of environment have been described which have implications for effective patterns of organization. Contingency theorists have also studied several dimensions of task. One of these, the interdependence among groups of an organization, stands out as being especially important for organizational design.[3]

The interdependence required to perform an organization's task is a variable which has been identified by several theorists as having implications for effective organization (Dill, 1958; Thompson, 1967; Lawrence and Lorsch, 1967; Galbraith, 1972; Lorsch and Allen, 1973). The work of Dill (1958), Gabarro (1971), and Lorsch and Allen (1973) suggest that the greater the interdependence required among subgroups of an organization, the lower the level of subgroup autonomy that is possible relative to the shared task. Thompson (1967) points out that the more complex the interdependence which an organization's task requires, the greater the difficulty and coordination costs of achieving integration among its subunits. Lorsch and Allen (1973) have also shown that organizations with tasks which require little interdependence between subunits employ simpler organizational structures and can rely more heavily on routinization of procedures than organizations with high interdependence. They found that the greater the required interdependence, the more elaborate were the integrating devices needed (such as task forces, committees, and coordinating departments) and the greater the effort expended to bring about integration.

The common theme of these studies is that the greater the interdependence required among subunits of an organization, the more difficult it is to achieve integration of effort and the more complex the integrating devices needed to bring about that integration.

## CONTINGENT DIMENSIONS OF ORGANIZATION

Before proceeding, it is worthwhile to briefly summarize several aspects of organization which stand out in the above review as being contingent on task or environment. The need for *differentiation* has been related to environmental diversity (the greater the diversity, the greater the degree of differentiation needed), and also to environmental change. The need for *integration* has been related to the interdependence required to perform an organization's task and meet environmental demands. The *difficulty* of achieving integration has been related to the degree of differentiation existing among subunits (and thus, indirectly to environmental diversity if subunits are interdependent). The difficulty of achieving integration has also been related to the intensity of interdependence. *Distribution of influence* has been related to all three environmental dimensions: environmental change, diversity, and uncertainty. The more turbulent the environment along any of these dimensions, the wider the distribution of influence required within the organization. *Subunit autonomy* has been identified as being contingent upon diversity, change, and interdependence. The more diverse the environment, the greater the discretion needed at the subunit level. The faster the change in the environment, the more autonomy that is needed. The greater the interdependence among subunits, the lower the autonomy that is possible with respect to the shared task.

Several of the dimensions reviewed earlier can be considered characteristic of an organization's formal structure.

*Formality of structure* has been related to uncertainty and rate of change such that the greater the uncertainty or change, the less formalized the appropriate structure. *Segmentation* has been described as being directly contingent on diversity. The need for *integrating* devices has been related to both interdependence and differentiation, so that the greater the interdependence or differentiation, the more extensive the need for integrating devices to facilitate integration of effort.

## ORGANIZATION VARIABLES WHICH ARE NOT CONTINGENT ON ENVIRONMENT OR TASK

The research reviewed thus far also suggests that two of the variables described earlier are not contingent on environment or task. These are (1) organizational norms about conflict resolution, and (2) the quality of integration which exists within the organization. It is especially important to identify these as noncontingent variables because they are often mistakenly thought of as depending on task or environment or are confused with variables which are contingent, such as the need for integrating devices, or the formality of structure.

The presence of open and confronting norms about conflict resolution has been identified by Lawrence and Lorsch (1967) as a shared characteristic of high-performing organizations in all of the environments they studied. These findings were consistent with the earlier work of Blake and Mouton (1964) and many others.

Similarly, their findings as well as those of Lorsch and Allen (1973) also suggest that high-performing organizations in all environments are characterized by greater integration than low-performing organizations. Thus, although the need for integration may vary with interdependence and the difficulty of achieving it may vary with differentiation and intensity of interdependence, the quality of collaboration itself is not a contingent variable. Obviously, there are many other characteristics of effective organizations which are not contingent on environment or task, but these two have been singled out because they are widely referred to within the contingency literature and as such may be mistakenly thought of as being contingent on environment or task.

## DIAGNOSING ORGANIZATION-ENVIRONMENT "FIT"

This brief review of contingency theory has attempted to describe several organizational variables that are contingent on environment and task dimensions. A number of empirical studies[4] have applied contingency theory to the school system setting, including urban school systems. The results of these studies suggest that these concepts can be usefully applied to diagnose organization-environment fit in the school system setting. The discussion thus far has not dealt with the specifics of diagnosing fit or the implications of such a diagnosis for OD training interventions. The purpose of this section is to describe some guidelines for conducting an environmental analysis as part of an OD program and for determining its implication for planned interventions within the system.

The experience of OD practitioners who have used contingency concepts in their work suggests a sequence of interrelated steps. (1) The initial scope and goals of the OD program are defined to include a concern with environmental needs and their implications for organization and behavior. (2) The OD specialists and relevant system personnel engage in a process of "scanning" the school systems environment. (3) This "scanning" activity leads to an identification of key constituencies, major issues, and the environmental needs which the system must meet to be effective. (4) An understanding of these needs and issues and a commitment to address them is obtained from the system's top administrative group. (5) A diagnosis is made by the OD team in conjunction with system personnel of the implications of environmental needs for organization and the extent to which the current organization is suited to meeting these needs. (6) Based on the organizational requirements identified in this diagnosis, implications are drawn for specific training interventions and organizational design changes. (7) The needed training interventions and organizational changes are made. (8) An ongoing process is established to monitor organization-environment fit and the effectiveness of interventions that are made as part of the OD program. This series of steps is meant to imply a general sequencing of phases in the OD effort. It is unlikely that they would occur in precisely that sequence in a typical OD effort. For example, it is reasonable to expect that a number of relevant training interventions will occur during the scanning and diagnosis stages because those very processes are apt to surface the need for problem-solving skills.

## SCANNING THE SYSTEM'S ENVIRONMENT

If an OD program is to deal with organization-environment fit, its goals must include, from the outset, a concern with environmental needs as they are related to internal behavior and organization. In simplest terms, this means that the initial goal-setting and data-gathering phases of an OD program should include an identification of important groups and forces in the system's environment, what demands and needs they pose for the organization, and what the system must do to meet these needs. This activity requires that the system's environment be systematically scanned and analyzed for the requirements it presents to the organization.

This scanning activity can occur in a combination of ways. The OD teams can gather data on the system's environment as part of the initial interviewing and observation. Information on the environment should also be gathered in group meetings of relevant system personnel as part of the early goal and issue identification stages of the program. It is also highly desirable that perceptions of important groups or organizations in the system's environment (including students and parents) be gathered as part of this process. Once the OD team and relevant system personnel agree on what the environmental needs and issues are, it is possible to identify what the organizational requirements are to meet these environmental demands.

**ANALYZING FIT**

Analysis of organization-environment fit at the systemwide level is done first by evaluating in general terms how well the current organization is suited to meeting environmental needs. This process can begin with an appraisal of the consonance between organizational characteristics and environmental traits at a general level.

The contingent relationships reviewed earlier in this article can all serve as initial guides for gauging overall organization fit. For example, if the system's environment is in the process of rapid and turbulent change, the organization's structure should be able to facilitate rapid decision-making and response and should minimize the number of levels in the hierarchy through which information must pass before decisions are made. Similarly, the capacity to resolve conflicts and solve problems becomes especially important, and a heavy reliance on rules and procedures is inappropriate. If the system's environment is highly diverse, it indicates a need for functional segmentation within the system; uniform procedures and rules cease to be universally applicable for all situations.

This initial appraisal of general organizational and environmental characteristics is useful as a first step. However, a much more detailed diagnosis of the implications of environmental demands is needed to identify what specific interventions should be made. This can be accomplished by focusing on organizational requirements in three areas: (1) the relationships required among parts of the system to meet environmental and task demands; (2) the relationships between the system and important groups in its environment; and (3) the overall appropriateness of the administrative organization given these environmental demands.

## Interunit Relations

Since the OD effort will focus on organizational variables, this section will describe several dimensions of interunit relationships which should be explored as part of the environment-organization analysis.

*Need for differentiation* can be indicated by environmental diversity, if different parts of the system relate to distinctly different parts of the environment, and if the nature of the needs posed by these subenvironments differs markedly. A need for differentiation can also be indicated if the environment is in a rapid state of change such that it poses a number of short-term crises for the system while also requiring that the system bring about major long-term changes.

At this time, existing diagnostic instruments are not reliable or inclusive enough to predict the need for differentiation in school systems (Gabarro, 1973). Therefore, the diagnosis of the need for differentiation must be carried out somewhat subjectively by the OD team personnel based on their knowledge and perceptions of environmental needs.

Since the need for differentiation does not lend itself to easy diagnosis, the OD team must consider environmental and task demands in fairly concrete terms. This can be done by asking such questions as what are the specific services which the system must provide to satisfy client needs. Do the needed services or activities require that different parts of the system (such as schoolhouses, curriculum services, and pupil services) develop different attributes, orientations, and goals? For example, in one school system, an environmental analysis indicated that if the system was to meet the needs of increasing minority enrollments, it had to bring about major changes in curricula and develop new programs and methods. However, it was also found that the central office curriculum services group had developed goal orientations and time orientations that were so similar to those of the schoolhouse staffs which they served that curriculum services personnel were focusing only on immediate curriculum needs and "fire-fighting" activities. As a result, the curriculum services group was not dealing with the larger and longer term needs of the schools. Such major curriculum changes as the development of a new career field, an intensive reading curriculum, or an early childhood program were all examples of major changes which no one single school could plan and implement by itself but which a curriculum services group could focus on and help develop. A curriculum services group which had a longer-term time orientation and a strong orientation to change could help assist schools accomplish these goals. Hence a need for greater differentiation existed which could have been detected by an OD team.

Similarly, in another school system, the needs of a changing pupil population required more and better services of an individual pupil nature. But it was discovered that pupil services personnel were spending much of their time performing administrative chores, such as checking on attendance and patroling halls. As a result they were not providing specialized services that were needed. In this case the pupil services group's concerns, goals and attitudes were so similar to those of schoolhouse administrators that the system was ineffective at dealing with individual pupil problems. A need clearly existed for greater differentiation between pupil services staff and schoolhouse administrators. An OD team could have made such a diagnosis and intervened to improve the situation.

*Need for integration* is indicated by the extent to which meeting environmental demands requires interdependence among parts of the school system. A diagnosis of the need for integration can be made by identifying which groups must collaborate in order for the system to meet environmental demands effectively.

Several instruments have been developed which can be used in diagnosing the need for integration. Schmuck and Runkel and their colleagues have developed a series of instruments which can be used to gauge the need for integration within an individual school (Schmuck et al., 1972: 146-150). Derr (1971) has developed an instrument which can be used to gauge the need for integration between the teaching, planning, and externally oriented subunits of a school system. Gabarro (1971) has developed an instrument to determine the interdependence between individual schools and several support groups, including curriculum services, pupil services, and special planning services.

In diagnosing the need for integration, an attempt should be made to identify the interdependencies which are critical to meeting environmental needs. One obvious example already cited is where meeting the needs of a changing pupil population requires major innovations or changes in curriculum. In this case, integration between schoolhouses and the curriculum services department becomes especially important.

Several instruments have been developed to diagnose the quality of integration or collaboration which actually exists between subunits of a system (Gabarro, 1971), or within an individual school (Schmuck et al., 1972). When used with interview and observation data, these instruments can be used to appraise the extent to which the need for integration is being met within the system.

*Subunit autonomy.* Both the review of the broader contingency literature and two studies of urban school systems (Gabarro, 1973, 1971; Derr, 1971) suggest that diagnosing the need for subunit autonomy requires care. Although a high rate of change or diversity in a system's environment would indicate a need for high subunit autonomy, this would not be the case if environmental demands also required a high degree of interdependence among the system's subunits (see in particular Gabarro, 1971, for a discussion of this situation). Where meeting environmental demands requires tight integration of effort among groups of a system (such as between individual schools and curriculum services groups), achieving this integration may act to reduce the autonomy traditionally enjoyed by subunits. This is because the mutual influencing required to achieve integration may result in subunits enjoying less autonomy vis-à-vis each other in relation to the shared task.

## Relationship Between the System and Groups in its Environment

An appraisal of client needs and values may also indicate that the traditional transactions of the system with groups in its environment are not sufficient for meeting those needs. When this occurs it is often because the vehicles used for bridging across the organization's boundary are no longer appropriate. For example, in some communities, PTA organizations do not provide adequate vehicles for reaching the mainstream of a school's parents or community. In other cases, community groups and parents may demand a more active voice in school policy than that offered by PTAs. In many urban areas today, community action groups are pressing for greater influence on school policy and programs. In several school systems with which the author has worked, these demands seemed especially deep-rooted because the communities were predominantly Black or Puerto Rican and many parents perceived the schools as being "white" institutions which were out of touch with their needs. In two of these school systems the administrations responded by establishing school-community councils which served as forums for direct input from parents and community groups and for mutual problem-solving. In both cases, these councils provided an organizational vehicle which could potentially improve the system's ability to identify and respond to client needs. One of these systems has subsequently enlarged the councils to include pupil membership.

The creation of such "bridging" organizations is not in itself sufficient, and its successful use requires that school staff have the skills and orientations to work productively with community groups (see the article by Schmuck in this issue). Such vehicles also expose the system to political struggles which may be taking place within the community. Like most structural changes that offer the potential of improving effectiveness by increasing interaction, devices of this kind require that system personnel develop a high level of interpersonal competence and problem-solving skills.

### Administrative Organization

The appropriateness of the system's administrative organization, will largely emerge from the detailed diagnosis of the issues just described. For example, the appropriateness of the administrative structure will depend in part on its ability to provide the integrating devices needed. It will also depend on the structure's capacity to facilitate decision-making. The distribution of influence within the organization (which may not necessarily reflect the formal organization chart) should also be explored by organizational members and the OD team to see whether influence resides where relevant information, competence, and contribution exist. This exploration can take place through interviews and group discussions of problem areas which usually surface issues about influence. Several instruments exist which can assist the OD team in making this diagnosis (see Tannenbaum, 1968; Lawrence and Lorsch, 1967).

## IMPLICATIONS FOR TRAINING INTERVENTIONS

The diagnosis just described will raise a number of implications for training interventions. Training interventions are especially important if it is determined that the system must achieve greater differentiation or tighter integration.

### DIFFERENTIATION

If the diagnosis suggests that differentiation should be maintained or increased, it is important that the OD effort assist organizational members in developing the interpersonal skills, norms, and conflict-resolving skills needed to function effectively within a differentiated system.

Experience suggests that as a first step it is essential that the system's top administrators truly understand why differentiation is needed and accept the need as legitimate. Otherwise, subsequent efforts to develop norms which support differentiation within the system are likely to fail. This is especially important for two reasons. First, and most importantly, greater differentiation will increase the potential level of interdepartmental conflict within the system (Lawrence and Lorsch, 1967; Walton and Dutton, 1967). Unless the top administrative group is aware of this possibility and understands its function, it will respond negatively to the emergence of this conflict. Second, many school systems actively socialize staff to believe that task orientations should not differ within the system, and that all groups should share the immediate goals and orientations of the classroom teacher. When this tradition exists in a system, it is especially critical that a sanction of legitimacy be given by the top administrators that it is all right for different groups to have different orientations.

*Norms which legitimate differences in orientation.* Once acceptance has been within the top administrative group, training interventions can be directed at developing norms which legitimate differentiation. It is likely that the very process of diagnosing organization-environment "fit" will act as an intervention in itself, particularly if it involves the active participation of system personnel at several levels. As Schein (1969) has pointed out, the data-gathering process is itself an intervention. The process of asking questions related to the need for differentiation will help create an awareness of differentiation, and its function.

Nonetheless, training interventions are needed to reinforce norms about the legitimacy of differentiation. Schmuck et al. (1972: 310-312) have described several ways in which training events can be designed to bring the need for both differentiation and integration into awareness and enable participants to experience them in small tasks. They have done this by designing training tasks in which differentiation and integration of activity is needed to complete the tasks effectively. They also suggest rotating combinations of trainees through the various subgroups that form during the training.

*Problem-solving and conflict-resolving skills.* Because differentiation can and does create potential conflict between departments and parts of the system, training interventions which focus on problem-solving and conflict-resolving skills are essential. Most OD designs would include this training as a central part of the program regardless of whether or not a need for differentiation is diagnosed. Training events with these purposes can be enhanced by making it explicit that differentiation is a functional source of conflict.

**INTEGRATION**

Like differentiation, a need for integration makes it especially important that training interventions be designed to develop strength in problem-solving and conflict-resolving skills. It is also necessary to prepare the way with early training events that help participants develop an awareness of why integration is needed. This is especially the case when the organization-environment diagnosis indicates an increased need for integration between different parts of a system. Historically, school systems dealing with stable environments have required very little interaction or integration between subunits (Bidwell, 1965; Lortie, 1969); and although intellectual awareness of the need for integration may come easily, an emotional commitment to what that means will come slowly.

The training events described by Schmuck et al. cited above can also serve as a means for building an awareness of the need for integration.

## IMPLICATIONS FOR ORGANIZATIONAL DESIGN

As the earlier review of contingency literature has pointed out, differentiation and integration have many implications for organizational structure and design.

*Integrating mechanisms.* If the diagnosis suggests that a high degree of integration is required among several subunits of a system (as, for example, between several schools and the central office curriculum services group or the pupil services group), then a need may exist for formal integrating devices to facilitate that integration. Several types of integrating devices can be used: interdepartmental task forces; integrating or coordinating roles; and integrating departments or groups such as program offices. Which of these mechanisms is appropriate depends on the importance and complexity of the interdependence, and the degree to which differentiation is required. For example, if a need for integration exists between several schoolhouses and the pupil services subgroup, then the use of a task force or coordinating committee may be useful and sufficient. Task forces of this nature have been used in several school systems as vehicles for setting priorities and resolving conflicts between pupil services and schools and as a channel through which principals can communicate their needs to pupil services administrators.

If a stronger need for integration exists, a person in an integrating role who is formally charged with facilitating collaboration may be required instead of, or in addition to, a task force. Such integrating roles are common in many urban systems. For example, a coordinator of middle school improvement was assigned in a school system which was attempting to bring about major changes in the curriculum of several of its middle schools. His purpose was to facilitate the planning and integration of effort that took place between staff in these schools and staff in several curriculum service groups. He was able to identify conflicts and help the schools and the curriculum services groups work together so that schoolhouse needs were being met.

Integrating departments or offices are the most complex (and costly) mechanisms for facilitating integration of effort. They are appropriate if a very high need for integration exists. One of the urban school systems studied by the author had developed an integrating department for elementary education and one for secondary education. The purpose of these groups was to facilitate integration of effort between schoolhouses and curriculum services personnel to bring about major curriculum change on a systemwide basis.

The need for and complexity of integrating devices depend on how important the interdependence is between subunits and how differentiated they are from each other. As with any organizational device, a change in structure or the creation of a formal role is not sufficient. It only offers the potential of facilitating integration. If the personnel in the integrating roles do not have the requisite skills at problem-solving, the creation of such devices may only result in increasing the system's costs and overhead, with no tangible benefits to either the organization or its clients.

*Administrative structure.* The implications of environmental needs for organizational structure have already been discussed under organization-environment fit. Any realistic redesign of an organization's structure must consider not only the task and environmental demands facing the organization, but also the key personnel in the system, their strengths and limitations, and the organizational histories of important subunits. Experience suggests that the implementation of structural changes are generally more successful if they occur during the later phases of an OD program. This gives organizational members time to develop skills and understanding which then reduce the threat and difficulties posed by the organization changes and improve their capacity to decide where changes are needed. It also provides the system and the OD specialists time to clarify important issues and needs, thereby improving the validity of the diagnosis.

## SOME CONCLUDING COMMENTS

### THE CONCEPT OF FIT IN PERSPECTIVE

Before concluding, it should be noted that the notion of organization-environment fit has been recently described as being a static concept. If the concept is viewed narrowly this might become the case, and it is therefore useful to clarify some of the assumptions implicit in the above discussion. In an important critique of contingency theory, Argyris (1972: 3-33) has made two major criticisms of the concept of fit:

(1) the basic idea of appropriate fit is a static concept in that it assumes that changes are not going to occur; and

(2) if changes in the environment do occur, it is assumed that the organization is able to shift its structure and behavior. The former may be possible, but the latter is questionable without major changes in variables such as the predispositions, attitudes, and interpersonal skills of organizational members.

Given these criticisms, it is important to identify where differences and similarities exist between the assumptions Argyris attributes to a contingency approach and those implicit in the approach advocated here.

The implicit assumption in the approach advocated in this paper is that changes in environment are very likely to occur, and for this reason is is especially important to consider environmental factors and their implications for organization. An institution which does not do this will not remain adaptive. Awareness of organization-environment fit is important because conditions do change, and what may have been appropriate at an earlier point in time may no longer fit current needs.

In the same vein, the approach advocated in this paper assumes that organizations are capable of changing their structure and behavior. Indeed, this is a major premise of organizational development. However, Argyris's point is quite valid in that such changes do not occur easily and cannot be arbitrarily mandated by administrators or consultants. He is also correct in saying that it is unlikely that either can change without the active involvement of organizational members and certainly not unless individual attitudes and interpersonal skills are seen as central factors. OD efforts are useful in facilitating organizational change because they consciously address these variables. For this reason, it has been the purpose of this paper to make explicit the relationship between organization-environment fit and organizational development.

It seems unlikely that Argyris's major quarrel is with the concept of contingency itself since he was among the first authors to suggest that different organizational forms are functional for different purposes (Argyris, 1964). Rather, his appears to be a much more basic concern. This concern is that organizations which are fitted to benign, stable environments lose their ability to be innovative and produce inflexible systems which are not apt to either "see" or adapt to change (Argyris, 1972). There is evidence to suggest that this is not an idle fear. The inability of many traditional school systems to adapt to increasing minority enrollments may be an illustration of this tendency. An awareness of this tendency becomes very important for systems operating in stable environments. If it is assumed that this tendency is real, school systems in stable environments must develop processes which allow them to consider issues and possibilities outside of their immediate environments. However, the overall usefulness of the notion of fit should not be discarded because this tendency exists in organizations adapted to stable conditions.

## SUMMARY

This article has attempted to describe several dimensions of organization-environment fit. It has also described some concepts which can be used in diagnosing the degree to which a school system's organization matches the demands and needs of its environment. Finally, it has attempted to present some implications of such a diagnosis for OD interventions.

Because of this purpose, the discussion has focused principally on environmental needs and their implications for organization. It has not dealt with several other important realities of organizations such as the organization's history, the needs and idiosyncracies of individuals in the organization, or important political and institutional constraints. The reader is asked to view the concepts and the approach described in this paper as a set of potentially useful tools for developing more effective and responsive organizations. Neither the concepts nor the approach offers a panacea or simple simple solution to the problems of urban education. Indeed, it is doubtful that any single technology or theory of OD is sufficient to address all of the complex reality of organizations. The process of better matching organization to environmental needs can substantially improve the effectiveness of OD efforts in urban school systems.

## NOTES

1. Some OD specialists, such as Lawrence and Lorsch (1969), base their entire approach on achieving a fit between an organization's structure and processes and its environment and member needs. More typical, however, are designs such as those described by Schmuck and Runkel and their colleagues, in which organization-environment fit is only one aspect of the program (Schmuck et al., 1972).

2. This is not an exhaustive summary of the factors identified in the Lawrence and Lorsch studies, but rather those which seem most relevant to urban school systems as organizations. The interested reader can find a more detailed review in Lawrence and Lorsch (1967).

3. Interdependence has been conceived of as a characteristic of task or technology by several authors (Woodward, 1965; Thompson, 1967; Perrow, 1967) and as an aspect of environmental requirements by others (Lawrence and Lorsch, 1967; Duncan, 1972). For purposes of this discussion it is thought of as a characteristic of an organization's task which is influenced by environmental demands, technology, and management's assumptions about how best to achieve the task.

4. For example, see Pusey, 1970; Hudson, 1971a, 1971b; Burnham, 1971; Gabarro, 1973, 1971; Derr, 1971. See in particular Derr and Gabarro (1972) for a critical review of this work as well as Campbell (1971) for a discussion of the difficulties of defining "environment" for school systems. An earlier work by Carlson (1964) is also germane in that it describes several idiosyncratic aspects of school system environments.

# REFERENCES

ALLEN, S. A., III (1970) "Corporate-divisional relationships in highly diversified firms," in J. W. Lorsch and P. R. Lawrence (eds.) Studies in Organizational Design. Homewood, Ill.: Richard D. Irwin.

ARGYRIS, C. (1972) The Applicability of Organizational Sociology. London: Cambridge Univ. Press.

——— (1964) Integrating the Individual and the Organization. New York: John Wiley.

BIDWELL, C. E. (1965) "The school as a formal organization," in J. G. March (ed.) Handbook of Organizations. Chicago: Rand McNally.

BLAKE, R. R. and J. S. MOUTON (1964) The Managerial Grid. Houston: Gulf.

BURNHAM, R. A. (1971) "Environmental and structural determinants of innovation in school districts." Presented at the meeting of the American Educational Research Association, February.

BURNS, T. and G. M. STALKER (1961) The Management of Innovation. London: Tavistock.

CAMPBELL, R. F. (1971) "Organization and Environment: a critique." Presented at the meeting of the American Educational Research Association, February.

CARLSON, R. O. (1964) "Environmental constraints and organizational consequences: the public school and its clients," in D. E. Griffiths (ed.) Behavioral Science and Educational Administration. Chicago: Univ. of Chicago Press.

DERR, C. B. (1971) "An organizational analysis of the _____ School System." Ph.D. dissertation. Harvard University.

——— and J. J. Gabarro (1972) "An organizational contingency theory for education." Educ. Administration Q. (Fall).

DILL, W. (1962) "The impact of environment on organizational development," in S. Marlick and E. H. Van Ness (eds.) Concepts and Issues in Administrative Behavior. Englewood Cliffs, N.J.: Prentice-Hall.

——— (1958) "Environment as an influence on managerial autonomy." Administrative Sci. Q. 2 (March).

DUNCAN, R. B. (1972) "Characteristics of organizational environments and perceived environmental uncertainty." Administrative Sci. Q. 17 (September).

EMERY, R. E. and E. L. TRIST (1965) "The casual texture of organizational environments." Human Relations 18 (February).

EVAN, W. (1966) "The organization-set: toward a theory of interorganizational relations," in J. Thompson (ed.) Approaches to Organizational Design. Pittsburgh: University of Pittsburgh.

GABARRO, J. J. (1973) "Organizational adaptation to environmental change," in F. Baker (ed.) Organizational Systems: General Systems Approaches to Complex Organizations. Homewood, Ill.: Richard D. Irwin.

——— (1971) "School system organization and adaptation to a changing environment." Ph.D. dissertation. Harvard University.

GALBRAITH, J. R. (1972) "Organizational design: an information processing view," in J. W. Lorsch and P. R. Lawrence (eds.) Organization Planning: Cases and Concepts. Homewood, Ill.: Richard D. Irwin.

GENTRY, J. E. and J. F. WATKINS (1973) "Organizational training for improving race relations." Auburn, Ala.: Auburn University School of Education. (unpublished)

HUDSON, B. M. (1971a) "Decentralization as a factor in educational adaptiveness: a theoretical explanation and a look at the Chilean experience." Ph.D. dissertation. Harvard University.

――― (1971b) "The D & I theory in a different culture." Presented at the meeting of the American Educational Research Association, February.

LAWRENCE, P. R. and J. W. LORSCH (1969) Developing Organizations: Diagnosis and Action. Reading, Mass.: Addison-Wesley.

――― (1967) Organization and Environment. Boston: Harvard University Graduate School of Business Administration Division of Research.

LEVINE, S. and P. WHITE (1961) "Exchange as a conceptual framework for the study of interorganizational relationships." Administrative Sci. Q. 5 (March).

LORSCH, J. W. and S. A. ALLEN III (1973) Managing Diversity and Interdependence: An Organizational Study of Multidivisional Firms. Boston: Harvard University Graduate School of Business Administration Division of Research.

LORTIE, D. C. (1969) "The balance of control and autonomy in elementary school teaching," in A. Etzioni (ed.) The Semi-Professions and Their Organization. New York: Free Press.

MORSE, J. J. (1970) "Organizational characteristics and individual motivation," in J. W. Lorsch and P. R. Lawrence (eds.) Studies in Organization Design. Homewood, Ill.: Richard D. Irwin.

PERROW, C. (1967) "A framework for the comparative analysis of complex organizations." Amer. Soc. Rev. 32 (April).

PUSEY, M. R. (1970) "Relating organizational theory to school systems in another culture (Australia)." Presented to the Harvard University Graduate School Education Committee on Degrees, February.

SCHEIN, E. H. (1969) Process Consultation: Its Role in Organization Development. Reading, Mass.: Addison-Wesley.

SCHMUCK, R. A., P. J. RUNKEL, S. L. SATUREN, R. T. MARTELL, and C. B. DERR (1972) Handbook of Organization Development in Schools. Eugene: University of Oregon Center for the Advanced Study of Educational Administration.

STARBUCK, W. H. (1965) "Organizational growth and development," in J. G. March (ed.) Handbook of Organizations. Chicago: Rand McNally.

TANNENBAUM, A. S. [ed.] (1968) Control in Organizations. New York: McGraw-Hill.

TERREBERRY, S. (1968) "The evolution of organization environments." Administrative Sci. Q. 12 (March).

THOMPSON, J. D. (1967) Organizations in Action. New York: McGraw-Hill.

WALTON, R. E. and J. M. DUTTON (1967) "The management of interdepartmental conflict: a model and review." Administrative Sci. Q. 14 (March).

WOODWARD, J. (1965) Industrial Organization: Theory and Practice. London: Oxford Univ. Press.

# DESIGNING CHANGE FOR EDUCATIONAL INSTITUTIONS THROUGH THE D/D MATRIX

ROBERT R. BLAKE
JANE SRYGLEY MOUTON
*Scientific Methods, Inc.*
*Austin, Texas*

**The behavioral sciences** have spawned a bewildering array of interventions calculated to change social practice. These interventions have spread through industry, government, medicine, and education not only in domestic situations but also internationally. Since each of these settings is unique to some degree, comparisons across settings are made increasingly more difficult. Yet there is so much variation within each of these institutional groupings that comparison of approaches even within a given setting is a virtual impossibility. Under these circumstances prospective users of behavioral science interventions have little more to go by than a subjective feel. Sticking a hand in and pulling "something" out of the behavioral science grab bag is a poor basis for being truly helpful in bringing about needed change.

But the situation is hopeless only at a phenotypical level. A genotypical approach does provide a basis for systematic ordering and comparison among these many and varied approaches and for evaluating their probable strengths and weaknesses. Thus a rational basis for the development of a science of change, rather than a trial-and-error basis for inducing change, becomes a practical possibility.

## THE D/D MATRIX®

This article introduces a framework for ordering the full range of behavioral science interventions that currently are being used or experimented with for changing social practices. It is referred to as the D/D Matrix, Figure 1, to emphasize the role of *diagnosis* and *development*. Examples are provided to indicate application possibilities to aid

| TYPES OF INTERVEN-TION | Unit of Change | | | | |
|---|---|---|---|---|---|
| | INDIVIDUAL | TEAM (group, project, department) | INTERGROUP (interdivisional, headquarters-field, union-management, etc.) | ORGANIZATION | SOCIETY |
| CATHARTIC | A | B | C | D | E |
| CATALYTIC | F | G | H | I | J |
| CONFRONTATION | K | L | M | N | O |
| PRESCRIPTIVE | P | Q | R | S | T |
| PRINCIPLES, MODELS, THEORIES | U | V | W | X | Y |

Figure 1: THE D/D MATRIX T.M.

educational administrators to evaluate approaches to planned change in a more insightful way.

Down the left side are five kinds of interventions. One is "Cathartic." This intervention helps a client sort out emotions in order to get a more objective view of his situation. The "Catalytic" intervention assists the client to collect and interpret data in order to get a better definition of his situation. A third, "Confrontation," challenges the client to evaluate how his unexamined values and assumptions may be coloring and distorting his views in ways that block effective action. A fourth kind of intervention is "Prescriptive." The prescriptive consultant tells the client what to do to solve his problem. A fifth approach to intervention involves the use of "Theory," "Principles," and "Models." By aiding the client to see his situation in systematic terms, he is enabled to diagnose his own situation in a more valid way and to convince himself as to what must be done to rectify the situation.

In any real-life situation, consultant interventions may be "pure" cathartic, "pure" catalytic, or "pure" confrontation, and so on. Some consultants employ "mixtures," taking a cathartic stance at one point, catalytic at another, confrontational at still another in a more or less unpredictable way. However, the majority appear to develop one major interventional style and to rely on it, sometimes to an excessive degree. The interventional approach employed should, of course, be based, not on what the consultant "wants" or "likes," but rather on what the client's system or situation needs in order for it successfully to come to grips with its problem.

Across the columns of the D/D Matrix are the targets of interventions. Historically, the most common behavioral science interventions have been with individuals, particularly in counseling and guidance and various approaches to rehabilitation and correction. Another unit of application may be the team—a small group of individuals who share an overriding responsibility for some activity. A school principal and those who report to him is an example. The super-intendent and his staff is another.

A third unit of application may be an intergroup relation-ship, for example, the relationship between two educational departments or between faculty and administration or between faculty and students. The organization as a whole is a fourth point of application, such as the school district or school building personnel or a university or a division such as the college of arts and sciences. Finally, larger *social systems*, such as community, city, or a sovercign state may be the target of behavioral science interventions.

These five kinds of interventions and five points of application make up into the 25-cell D/D Matrix. The letters in the cells identify the particular intervention being dis-cussed.

In what follows, we have sought to reduce the use of emotionally toned words for "who" does the intervening by making consistent use of the word "consultant" to replace any number of other words that might have been used— psychiatrist, counselor, trainer, helper, social worker, teacher, nun, pastor, and sometimes even confidant or colleague. By the same token the word "client" is used when referring to the unit of application whether it is an individual, team, organization, and so on. Rather than depicting an application example from each of the 25 cells, it will only be possible to provide one or two indications per row. Examples at the team, intergroup, and organizational levels rather than examples that deal with individuals are presented, on the premise that the reader is more likely to be familiar with interventions with individuals.

## CATHARTIC INTERVENTIONS

Being able to take an objective view of a situation, or of oneself, or of both, is essential for solving many problems. Taking an objective view can be made more difficult than the situation warrants, however, when emotions color "what is going on." Frustrations, anger, anxiety, even vague feelings that something is "wrong" can block the kind of thinking necessary for solving problems.

The core idea of cathartic interventions is that of a process of "cleansing" that brings about a release from tensions. Not all kinds of interventions promote catharsis. It takes a particular kind. With individuals such interventions are nonevaluative, supporting, encouraging, and inviting the client to talk more and express his feelings. Breaks in the flow of conversation involving gaps of silence are understood for what they are: as indicating points of impasse that the client must be given the opportunity to solve by the consultant's reacting in a patient and supportive way rather than being rushed over them. These are the basic attitudes behind the cathartic intervention. There are many human skills involved that have been illuminated in the technical literature. These are skills of rephrasing, reflecting, communicating acceptance by posture, gesture, smile, and others.

Many readers will recognize that cathartic interventions with individuals, located in Cell A, are in the tradition of client-centered, or nondirective counseling of the kind originated by Rogers with college students and brought to a high degree of refinement by Axline (1947) with children. In the industrial field this kind of cathartic intervention was launched in the thirties by Dickson and Roethlisberger (1966) for aiding workers to deal with their emotional involvements in ways that permitted them to increase their performance effectiveness. Because these are well known, they will not be commented upon further.

At the other end of the scale, in a Cell D intervention with an organization, the consultant continues to be no more evaluative, no less supportive, and no more controlling. But he is more active in the sense of creating a climate where participants can share with one another their tensions, frustrations, angers, and so on, and then talk about them and work them through.

Gibb (1972) describes such an intervention utilized with a total faculty of a small university at various times over a period of four years. His thesis is that organization life is fear-provoking and characterized by high levels of distrust and closedness among the people. As a result, they interact according to "role requirements" rather than out of spontaneity or problem-solving opportunities. His approach enables participants to experience and share with one another their community relatedness. The process is led by the consultant who works with participants who are congregated in an open place like a gym so that each can directly experience all of the others simultaneously without the encumbrances of chairs, tables, and so on. Nonverbal exercises engage participants in relating to one another in physical ways that serve to reduce inhibitions and closedness. These extend through a large number of activities, from several people collaborating to lift and rock another person, for example, to feeling the contours of an unidentified person while blindfolded, or one person leading a blindfolded person on a walk, with the sighted person helping the other person to experience his surroundings by smell, feel, and touch rather than through words or sight. Engaging in activities such as these "automatically" communicates a sense of closeness and mutual dependence. Because they occur in an open place, these activities can produce a contagion effect, with aroused emotions more easily expressed, talked about, and worked through. Gibb describes human values that are congruent with this emotionally freeing kind of intervention. Included are deep interpersonal acceptance as indicated by such words as being personal, people-oriented, intimate, and close. Individuals become more authentic, transparent, honest, available, and direct. Rather than controlling others, individuals become more allowing, less intrusive, less manipulative, more collaborative, and more sharing. He concludes that through such organization-building experiences, it is possible to use the climate of high trust and acceptance produced for problem-solving activities which continue to be carried out on an each-to-all, one community-wide setting.

In describing the impact of such an organization-building experience on a faculty, Gibb (1972: 121) described the faculty as more "close-knit," although not so much "student-oriented." Certain faculty members felt more free or able to "do their own thing," particularly in that they felt it was not necessary to deal with students in such a paternalistic way. Teachers, in the classroom, varied. Some were more participative while others preferred the more formal arrangements. He concludes that the faculty has not extended this kind of organization-building experience as yet to include the entire student body.

The key to understanding a cathartic intervention no matter whether the client is an individual, a team, an intergroup, an organization, or larger social system is the same. When the emotions and feelings that are hampering performance or disturbing behavior can be experienced, expressed, talked about, discussed, and "worked through," it then is more likely that an objective, problem-solving approach can be taken.

## CATALYTIC INTERVENTIONS

When added to certain other substances, a catalytic agent in its physical science meaning is something which causes a change in the speed of a chemical reaction. The change would not have occurred had this agent not been present.

The term has been used to describe one way of bringing change about in human situations. A consultant enters a situation with the intention of increasing the rate at which an already present "process" is occurring within the status quo. His goal is to assist those within the status quo to be more effective—doing what they are already engaged in, but in a better manner.

Two related but different basic assumptions underlie the catalytic intervention. One is that additional "data" are needed in order that a significant impact can occur in changing the rate of what is going on. Whatever is preventing problem-solving from being of a higher quality can be reduced by utilizing information that is available but that for some reason is not being brought to bear on the particular dilemmas at hand. The second aspect of a catalytic intervention focuses on procedures that the client is using in approaching his problems. These interventions may involve a given individual in an examination of his own thinking, or it may result in a number of people engaging in deliberations about the character of their teamwork, intergroup contacts, organizationwide activities, and so on. The consultant may seek to change the rate of progress through making either one or both of two kinds of contributions. The resultant activities usually are understandable to the client without further "education," though some skill practices may be used to get the client started.

Those in academic guidance work will recognize the catalytic aspects of student guidance as a Cell F example. After an interview to identify the student's problem, the consultant often provides a series of tests. Then he sits with the student to aid him in interpreting the meaning of scores. This is done by providing norms that indicate how much alike or different the student's interests or abilities are from the expressed interest or abilities of successful people in various pursuits or walks of life. The consultant avoids participating in the student's decisions about what he should or should not do. Rather his contribution is through giving procedural suggestions about how the data can be used and interpreted so the client can reach his own conclusions. There are many excellent examples of this (Patterson, 1973: 6-48).

Cell G interventions have become popular in recent years, particularly with the advent of catalytic team-building. As will be seen this has striking parallels with the approach to data-based guidance as reviewed in Cell F. Team-building often begins with the consultant interviewing to get a sense of problems as seen through the eyes of individual team members. Then he may design an additional data-gathering program based upon questionnaires, scales, and instruments in order to get a more accurate portrayal of the situation. Feedback is through returning the data, either in a raw form or only slightly categorized to the team itself and facilitating the "processing" of the data by sitting with the group as its consultant-facilitator. This sequence of activity is frequently concluded by the team drawing action implications and designing concrete programs of change. Since excellent descriptions of the catalytic approach to team-building are available in work by Miles et al. (1971), it will not be commented upon further.

H Cell interventions are calculated to improve intergroup relationships. An example is the following which involved relationships between students and faculty. Thirty-five students and faculty from a large high school convened on a self-selecting basis. During the first two days they exchanged reactions, experiencing a version of sensitivity training and group dynamic experiences. Both were involved for the purpose of improving communication through reducing status barriers and increasing the ease with which information could flow. Thereafter, assembled in small groups, usually on a mixed basis with both students and faculty in the same groups, these groups were then able to discuss conflicts existing within the school and among various groups and to consider constructive actions that might be taken. This approach has an important catalytic element because students and faculty were grouped together in the introductory period under a "shared" learning experience that permitted a free exchange over neutral content prior to discussing problems that existed in the school. This method of training in communication and group dynamics promoted the exchange and interpretation of "data." The likelihood of confrontation was low on any account, partly because of the self-selection basis for participation and partly because since neither students nor faculty were participating as representatives of the larger group from which they came, they could be more flexible and accommodating without being judged "traitors" or "turncoats" (Chesler and Lohman, 1971: 200-202).

One of the clearest expositions of a Cell I intervention is provided by Miles and Lake (1967). It contains striking parallels to catalytic interventions with individuals and teams. They describe a sequence of steps that reveal how the catalytic assumptions would work in a change effort involving an entire school organization. First, interviews are employed to clarify expectations and to gather data about existing attitudes, needs, interests, and problems. This step is followed by questionnaire-based data-gathering throughout the school. Then some focal group meets with the consultant and processes the data to interpret its meaning in terms of goals, attitudes, and beliefs, to see how different groups compare with one another and to create a priority listing of problems for the solution. The focal group, which is a steering committee, uses what it learns as a "mirror" against which to evaluate its own operations and to identify alternative improvement possibilities. In turn, the focal group exercises initiative by helping other groups to engage in the same kind of sequence of steps. Finally, structures and procedures are recommended to ensure institutionalization of these self-renewing procedures. The consultants then "phase out" of their facilitating roles, but continue to gather data which is fed back into the system and interpreted against data gathered in the beginning so that a pre-post evaluation of progress and new directions can take place. Schein's (1969) description of process consultation rests on similar catalytic assumptions.

A related kind of Cell I intervention is by Schmuck et al. (1971), who dealt with the entire faculty and supporting staff of one school organization—54 participants in all. A six-day interpersonal laboratory in which participants developed problem-solving skills was followed by "booster-shot" sessions during the school year. Process consultants, one working with each of the five groups, provided major facilitative interventions that assisted their learning through feeding back process observations as well as suggesting skill development activities that could reinforce new behavior. Two of the days of the interpersonal laboratory involved structured group exercises which had as their purpose to demonstrate, through first-hand data-gathering, the importance of clear communication and to "test" the experience for its pertinence in dealing with real-life problems. The last four days entailed a problem-solving sequence that might be employed back in the school system to approach the solution of real problems. It resulted in (1) identifying the problem, (2) completing a force field diagnosis, (3) brainstorming for reducing restraining forces, (4) designing steps to solve the problem, and (5) simulating the solution's soundness. This activity has operational impact, including (1) an increase in classroom application projects, (2) increased influence from an advisory committee on school operations, (3) improved relationships among faculty and administrators, (4) setting up an internal catalytic kind of facilitator to serve as a liaison, and other indicators of effect.

A third example of how a catalytic approach to organization-building can take place is offered by McElvaney and Miles (1971). Again it was started with interviewing, which was quickly followed by data-gathering from participants themselves. These data were then fed back with process consultation provided to aid participants to understand the meaning of their data. They observed their own interactions and shared interpersonal data as another basis for increasing their own effectiveness. This was followed by particular problems being assigned to specific task forces with next-step planning for future meetings. The catalytic character of the process consultation in this study is pictured in the consultant's own self-description which follows—a self-description based upon what participants said about him:

He's observant; he steps in and quizzes us on what we mean. He gets things straight. He's a catalyst between the administrators and the principals. . . . He's done a fine job of directing and redirecting the group's thinking towards specific goals [McElvaney and Miles, 1971: 132].

In a final example of a Cell I intervention, Derr (1970) has provided a case study where the "client" was fourteen special service departments in a big city school system. Initial entry was a problem because the school system was defensive about outsiders. A two-month delay occurred even before exploratory meetings between the consultants and school officials took place. Eventually data-gathering, through 24 interviews, got underway, with interviewees representing a diagonal slice of the organization. Senior school officials took no active part. As is true in catalytic consultation, these consultants were committed to confidentiality of interviewee sources but they identified four perceived problem areas including (1) poor coordination, (2) inadequate communication, (3) poor adaptation, and (4) destructive power struggles. Data feedback on their findings occurred with department heads but not with top members of the organization who requested and received a written report. Thus, the data feedback and process consultation features of a "standard" catalytic consultation were bypassed. A year later the original interviewees were reinterviewed. The conclusions drawn were that the feedback sessions had been a useless exercise since no change in capacity to exert upward influence had occurred during the interim. The same problems as previously existed remained unsolved.

The catalytic approach to intervention, whether with an individual, a team, an intergroup, an organization, or a larger social system, is premised upon the following. The consultant enters the situation and through interviewing gathers information about interests, needs, and problems as they are seen by the client. He then designs a data-gathering program and implements it, completing this phase of the intervention by feeding back to the client raw or categorized data. While the client is processing the data, the applied behavioral science consultant provides process consultation, which means that he facilitates the client's efforts to understand the data and to take action upon the basis of it. He may do this in two ways. One way is through technical aspects of data interpretation. The other way is through aiding the client to learn to be more effective in terms of sound behavior. The expected outcomes are that the client will (1) see his situation in a more objective way, (2) comprehend the actions necessary for increasing the effectiveness of his situation, and (3) have better interpersonal and decision-making skills with which to implement desired outcomes.

## CONFRONTATION

Sometimes the values and assumptions a client embraces must be brought to a plane of awareness in order for him to break out of self-defeating or ineffective behavior situations. The confrontational consultant's purpose is to face the client with contradictory, inappropriate, invalid, or unjustified assumptions, often revealed in his "here-and-now" behavior, in such a way as to aid the client to gain an explicit understanding of what these are and, at the same time, to see optional values and assumptions which, if he were to act on them, would increase effectiveness.

Confrontation involves challenging, and in this way getting the client to face up to a reality which previously was unrecognized, ignored, disregarded, or rejected. By such interventions the consultant seeks to create a sense of discrepancy, a contradiction between (1) values or assumptions that are valid in the light of research-based behavioral science findings or justifiable against some general philosophy, and (2) the actual values and assumptions that are operating within the client's situation. Many such basic values and assumptions are deeply embedded and difficult to get at. This is because they constitute second-nature "truisms," not themselves subject to being challenged and often not even recognized as such by the person who holds them. Under these conditions, when challenged a client is likely to engage in a variety of defensive practices which protect the embedded assumptions from scrutiny. However, a confrontational intervention approach takes this into account, and "stays with" the client until he recognizes the reality of his situation.

There are examples of confrontational interventions in which the client is an individual. Psychoanalysis is the outstanding example, but there are many others. Ellis's (1962) rational-emotive therapy is a case in point. The Gestalt approach to therapy is another (Herman, 1972). The confrontational consultant in each case sees it as his objective to engage the client, by challenge, interpretation, or by "forcing" the examination of a contradiction, to see that problems encountered are related to the assumptions that he holds. The route to increasing effectiveness is to rid himself of unjustified assumptions and replace them with more valid ones.

Team confrontations are also well known, particularly as they relate to exceptional behavior, such as the Synanon approach to drug addiction. In a Synanon community, there are two basic sets of values and assumptions. One set involves how participants are expected to carry out the work of the community. These are norms for diligence, cooperation, hard work, mutual support, and so forth. Another set of norms is involved among Synanon participants when they are in the "Game." When engaged in the Game, nothing—in word, action, or deed—is taken for granted or at face value. How a person explains, justifies, or rationalizes what he says, thinks, believes, or does is subject to challenge, confrontation, and contradiction. In addition, any behavior of a person playing the Game that has been observed in his wider Synanon community activities can be brought up by any other Game member to face that person with, to ensure that he recognizes a contradiction between what he verbally assents to and what he factually does in his everyday behavior.

Other group-level confrontations are involved in the psychoanalytic approach to group therapy as demonstrated by Ezriel (1950), or in industrial contexts as demonstrated by Argyris (1970).

Intergroup relationships may be in a state of tension, antagonism, and win-lose, such as was true in the late sixties between school administrators and students. Such disturbed relationships may be between two departments in a university, such as between the department of psychology and of educational psychology, applied mathematics and "pure" mathematics, or biochemistry and chemistry. A confrontational intervention is a way of bringing the issues of controversy to focus and resolution.

An approach to improving student and faculty relationships of a confrontational character, was experimented with in a New Jersey workshop. It was based on the assumption that each group—students and faculty—has its own motivations and, in addition, each may see the other quite differently than either group sees itself. Getting these perceptions identified and communicated between groups while preserving the integrity of both sides, was built into the intervention.

Students and teacher groups were separated and each asked to develop a list of ways they saw the other. Some of the phrases used by students to picture teachers included

Unaware, think they are correct because they are older, some making honest effort, take things personally, don't really listen, are prejudiced.

In contrast among the characteristics teachers reported regarding students were

Cherish individuality, hopelessness, confusion, self-confidence, frustration, sensitivity, eagerness, resistance to seeing both sides of the question, clannish, irresponsible, candid, bored, angry at inequities, flexible, racially polarized [Chesler and Lohman, 1971: 201].

After each group had worked in isolation from the other and had produced these images, there was an exchange of images across groups in a public meeting. While both sets of images contain valid elements, a neutral observer might very well conclude that each group's image of the other was "distorted" by virtue of the membership characteristics of the group who formed them. The confrontational consultant may have intervened on the assumption that subjective elements in these images, which are not necessarily recognized by those who hold them, need to be emphasized and understood. By resolving such mutual misunderstandings, a prerequisite for realistic problem-solving collaboration has been met. In this case study, the initial response to the approach was positive, but as the school year wore on, collaborative efforts ended for reasons that are not explained.

These examples characterize a confrontational approach to diagnosis and development. It rests on the assumption that values and assumptions held by the client that influence his behavior in significant ways may be invalid or unjustified. It is unlikely that significant shifts in effectiveness will result until he becomes aware of what these assumptions are and has the opportunity to examine alternative possibilities. Thus, the role of a confrontation is to ensure that unexamined values and assumptions are identified and evaluated and when found unacceptable replaced by values and assumptions that have a stronger base of validity, judged against research-based behavioral science criteria.

## PRESCRIPTION

Prescriptions are well-known and time-honored approaches for dealing with problems. The medical model is the best known. Once the doctor completes his diagnosis, he tells the patient his answer: what the patient needs to do or what needs to be done, including what treatment, if any, will help him to regain health.

The prescriptive consultant in an analogous fashion relies on skills acquired from a body of knowledge or from years of practical experience. He operates on the premise that he is well qualified to discern the client's true needs. By definition the client himself lacks the requisite knowledge or the objectivity or both to make a sound self-diagnosis. Thus, a prescriptive consultant, once he has identified what the real problem is, tells the client what actions would be necessary to take to bring the problem under control or toward resolution. A significant feature is that prescriptions are possible even when the client is at his wit's end, or has thrown his hands up in despair.

There are numerous examples of Cell P interventions. The Alcoholics Anonymous approach is of a prescriptive character, although it also contains confrontational as well as catalytic and cathartic elements. It is prescriptive because the individual member who joins AA is often at his wit's end. He surrenders himself by accepting the premise that through reliance on outside authority and by giving up his will to control himself, he will be able to gain the strength necessary for coping with his problem.

Other prescriptive approaches are found throughout humanistic psychology and the encounter movement. An example is one that occurred in a marathon group situation. Claire, a young girl, had come to the session at the suggestion of her therapist. She indicated to other members that her problem involved her reluctance to accept dates. When invited to do so, she did not know how to act. She thought of herself as unfeminine, felt awkward, and was not often asked out a second time. The prescriptive approach presumed that Claire needed directiveness and support from a "mother-kind" of person. The marathon leader took Claire by the hand. They went around the group, speaking to each of the men in turn in a flirtatious manner. Claire's initial reaction was that this would not be something she could do, but by a little prescriptive "push" she tried. Each time that she spoke to one of the men, she received a compliment for the attractiveness with which she conducted herself. By the end of the session she felt much freer. By telling her what to do and supporting her while she did it, she had been helped to "reality-test" and thereby to solve her problem (Mintz, 1971: 19-21).

Approaches to desensitization, increasingly popular in high school, such as by Wolpe (1968, 1958) and Wolpin (1968), are also premised on the consultant interacting with the client in a prescriptive orientation. The client carries out the assigned exercise involving doing in imagination what the client fears to do in real life. As a result, he gains the ability to engage in activities which previously were so frightening or threatening as to be avoided.

Interventions that also are of a prescriptional character are involved in some approaches to behavior modification, such as by Krumboltz (1965). The consultant only agrees to go forward once he has a contract with the student to engage in the special activity. Then the activity is designed by the consultant and the reward system for positive behavior on the part of the client is retained in the consultant's control.

Prescriptional interventions in Cell R are ones that involve two groups that are blocked by unresolvable controversy. By bringing in a third person to act as a neutral judge and arbitrator, a prescriptive approach to solution is relied upon. Once both sides of the issue have been heard, the arbitrator makes a ruling. Acceptance of his ruling by both groups is expected, and it is final and binding.

To summarize: a prescriptive consultant is involved in "telling" the client what to do and often in supervising him while executing the consultant's plan.

## THEORY, PRINCIPLES, AND MODELS

The fifth row of the D/D Matrix involves interventions that rest on "teaching" the client theories, or principles, or how to design models. Thereafter the consultant helps the client use these theories, principles or models as the basis for diagnosing his situation and for designing developmental strategies for increasing his effectiveness. The idea is that when a problem can be seen and comprehended in systematic terms involving cause and effect, it can be responded to in ways which get at the root of the problem. Theory, principles, and models, in other words, are ways of bringing systematic analysis to bear on diagnosis and solution of problems—human or physical—in comparison with reliance on hunch, intuition, "common sense," or tradition-based wisdom. Once the client has the insights and understandings that theories, principles, and models pertinent to his situation can produce, he has a mature basis for self-reliance.

The use of the theory-principles-models basis needs to be distinguished from other approaches that might be confused with it. For example, consultation approaches described earlier involving either catharsis, catalysis, or confrontation, may be ones in which the consultant is crystal clear about the theory behind his intervention. However, he does not teach the theory to the client. This does not involve theory, principles, or models consultation because the *client* does not learn theories, principles, or models. In addition, many times the word "theory" is used loosely to mean a frame of reference, or to be equivalent to the word "assumption," or to represent a "cognitive map." These are not theories in the more rigorous behavioral science meaning, but rather may represent little more than common-sense explanations for what is happening in a situation.

The Grid® diagram in Figure 2 provides an example for seeing Blake and Mouton's (1964, 1962) use of theory as an intervention: 9,1 is a hard, directive, controlling approach; 1,9 is a soft, smoothing, acceptance approach; 1,1 is a neutral, indifferent, withdrawn approach; 5,5 is an accommodating, compromising, adusting, organization-man, bureaucratic approach; 9,9 is an open, confronting, authentic, excellence-motivated approach. McGregor's (1960)

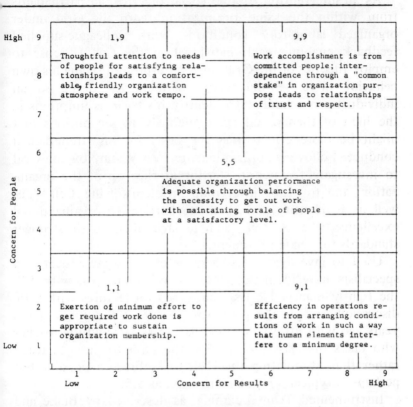

SOURCE: Reprinted by permission from The Managerial Grid, by Robert R. Blake and Jane Srygley Mouton. Houston: Gulf Publishing Co., 1964, page 10.

Figure 2: THE GRID®

Theory X corresponds with 9,1; and Theory Y is a mixture of 9,9, 5,5, and 1,9 elements. Likert's (1967) System 4 is more akin to 5,9 and his System 1 to 9,1. McClelland's (et al., 1953) Need Achievement often is interpreted as pushing people in a 9,1 direction and Herzberg's (et al., 1959) motivational theories, on the hygienic side, seem open to 1,9 interpretation and use; whereas on the recognition-achievement side they are more related to 9,9.

As an intervention to alter social practice, all participants from within the same organization learn the Grid under organized laboratory conditions, with colleague-supplied feedback enabling each individual in the Cell U sense to employ theories of the Grid for the purpose of seeing his own behavior in a self-diagnostic manner. By doing so an individual can be aided to identify his basic assumptions in the light of theory and simultaneously to see options that might be more effective as the basis for his strengthened conduct. Followup applications, in Cell V, employ the Grid to investigate teamwork, starting at the top of the organization, and to probe intergroup problem-solving, Cell W, as well as to identify and eliminate barriers to organizational excellence, the X cell, and replace them with stronger standards for accomplishment.

Used to investigate classroom practices, some educational specialists have identified "permissive" education with 1,9; the tightly managed classroom, based on lectures with little discussion, as 9,1; the professor who reads the notes of ten years ago with little voice modulation as 1,1; and the teacher who takes the class "tempo" as the basis for how to teach rather than stimulating the class to embrace a possible but perhaps untypical tempo and quality, as 5,5.

Instrumented Team Learning, as described by Blake and Mouton (1962), and some approaches that involve "proactive" and "discovery" learning, may rest on 9,9 elements.

The use of theory, principles, and models for intervening to increase the effectiveness of practice has advanced at a far more rapid rate in industry and government than it has in education. The reasons for this are difficult to understand. According to stereotypes of the day it might be expected that educators would be the first to utilize theory because of their understanding of its power to explain phenomena in its scientific application, and businessmen the last to do so because of their "hard facts" empiricism, which says, in effect, "if it works, do it and don't ask questions."

Except for use of the Grid, there are few good examples of the theory, principles, and models mode of intervention in educational settings. One use of the Grid, however, can be summarized (Blake and Mouton, 1966, unpublished). Forty participants, two-thirds of whom were school administrators and the remainder teachers in a suburban city of moderate size, learned the Grid in a week-long seminar. Included among them were several who were members of the school board, superintendents, principals and their assistants, and counselors from the various junior high schools, high schools, and so on. There were also participants who represented the tax assessor's office.

Participants learned the Grid and practiced skill in using it with one another for feedback and self-examination. Data resulting from this Grid seminar for educators can be compared with comparable data from population of industrial personnel. Here are some conclusions drawn from this comparison. In the comparison between industrial personnel and school people, the educational personnal (a) judged themselves to be more 5,5; (b) rejected 9,1 more strongly as a self-description; (c) embraced 1,9 more strongly as a self-judgment; and (d) rejected 1,1 less often as a self-description. When actual team effectiveness in finding "best" solutions to set problems in small study teams were compared, school people were far less competent in finding "best" solutions. They lacked teamwork skills, being too ready to resolve differences by voting or "following" the "official leader."

These conclusions represent only one school system, and therefore they should be regarded as suggestions rather than definitive. However, they suggest important implications. They point to an organization-man, bureaucratic, mechanistic, and compromising basis for dealing with problems. These are the attitudes that lead to acceptance of the status quo or a more or less "as is" basis in preference to embracing standards of excellence.

Now, it is possible to reexamine a statement made earlier, to the effect that educational institutions have made little use of the theories, principles, or models mode of intervention. Our view would be that theories, principles, or models as an intervention basis are seen by people in a bureaucratic orientation as being too demanding of learning and too remote from the everyday momentary realities to be worth "the effort." Rather, the catalytic approach of interviewing and using survey research with feedback and process consultation makes empirical data available with minimum personal effort or commitment. This provides a basis for understanding why the catalytic interventions described earlier have for the most part had such relatively little effect. Indeed, Schmuck and Miles (1971), in the preface of their book, conclude that, after almost a decade of educational interventions there were only five active organization-building experiments within educational settings in the United States.

## SUMMARY AND IMPLICATIONS

The field of education can become a major setting for behavioral science interventions.

The reader may have been struck with the fact that cathartic and catalytic interventions are the most common. The cathartic interventions provide a basis for emotional release and sharing and in that sense create circumstances favorable to the renewal of problem-solving activity. The catalytic kind of intervention, on the other hand, promotes information-gathering, data-sharing, and empiricism. It is the more popular of the two. This view also is held by Schmuck and Miles (1971: 9-23), who acknowledge that approaches that are characterized here as cathartic are "soft" interventions and that they have been the most common in school settings.

Both the cathartic and the catalytic approaches are, in our view, too weak to create much deep or lasting impact on school systems. Both are premised on accepting and working with "felt" needs of administrators, faculty, and students within the status quo. In a real sense, though in an unwitting way, both kinds of interventions are comfortable. They may "collude" with inherent school system weaknesses of the sort characterized as involving organization-man, bureaucratic, mechanistic, and compromising approaches.

The impact that can be expected from confrontational approaches is stronger, but if their absence from the literature can be taken as an indicator, they are probably seen as too "abrasive" to be acceptable. By virtue of the fact that prescriptive interventions give "answers," it is probable that they too are seen as too arbitrary to be very acceptable.

Approaches premised on organization members' learning theories, principles, and models, employed for self-diagnosis as a first step and followed by team-building, intergroup problem-solving, and the setting of organization goals of excellence, also were found to be rare in this survey of behavioral science interventions within educational settings. This rarity was interpreted as related to the possibility that theory is seen as "remote" and "distant," rather than as immediate and useful. In any contrast of the desirability of the catalytic with the theories, principles, and models approach, the catalytic approach is possibly accepted because it is more congenial to the bureaucratic, mechanistic, compromising orientation thought to be more prominent in school systems than in industrial corporations. Looking beyond the present, the D/D Matrix provides the academic administrator and faculty member as well a systematic basis for ordering the behavioral-science-based choices available for strengthening the effectiveness of individuals, teams, intergroup relationships, organizations as unities, and larger social systems.

# REFERENCES

ARGYRIS, C. (1970) Intervention Theory and Method. New York: McGraw-Hill.

AXLINE, V. M. (1947) Play Therapy. Boston: Houghton Mifflin.

BLAKE, R. R. and J. S. MOUTON (1966) Records of a laboratory conducted for a client of Scientific Methods, Inc. (unpublished)

——— (1964) The Managerial Grid: Key Orientations for Achieving Production Through People. Houston: Gulf.

——— (1962) "The instrumented training laboratory," in Series Five of Issues in Human Relations Training, NTL Selected Readings.

CHESLER, M. A. and J. E. LOHMAN (1971) "Changing schools through student advocacy," in R. A. Schmuck and M. B. Miles (eds.) Organization Development in Schools. Palo Alto, Calif.: National Press Books.

DERR, C. B. (1970) "Organization development in one large urban school system." Education and Urban Society 2, 4: 403-419.

DICKSON, W. J. and F. R. ROETHLISBERGER (1966) Counseling in an organization: A sequel to the Hawthorne investigations. Cambridge, Mass: Harvard University Graduate School of Business Administration Division of Research.

ELLIS, A. (1962) Reason and Emotion in Psychotherapy. New York: Lyle Stuart.

EZRIEL, H. (1950) "A psycho-analytic approach to group treatment." British J. of Medical Psychology 23: 59-74.

GIBB, J. R. (1972) "The TORI community experience as an organizational change intervention," pp. 109-126 in W. W. Burke (ed.) Contemporary Organizational Development: Conceptual Orientations and Interventions. Washington, D.C.: NTL Institute for Applied Behavioral Science.

HERMAN, S. M. (1972) "A Gestalt orientation to organization development," pp. 69-89 in W. W. Burke (ed.) Contemporary Organization Development: Conceptual Orientations and Interventions. Washington D.C.: NTL Institute for Applied Behavioral Science.

HERZBERG, F. et al. (1959) The Motivation to Work. New York: John Wiley.

KRUMBOLTZ, J. D. [ed.] (1965) Revolution in Counseling: Implications of Behavioral Science. Boston: Houghton Mifflin.

LIKERT, R. (1967) The Human Organization: Its Management and Value. New York: McGraw-Hill.

McCLELLAND, D. A. et al. (1953) The Achievement Motive. New York: Appleton-Century-Crofts.

McELVANEY, C. T. and M. B. MILES (1971) "Using survey feedback and consultation," pp. 113-138 in R. A. Schmuck and M. B. Miles (eds.) Organization Development in Schools. Palo Alto, Calif.: National Press Books.

McGREGOR, D. (1960) The Human Side of Enterprise. New York: McGraw-Hill.

MILES, M. B., P. H. CALDER, H. A. HORNSTEIN, D. M. CALLAHAN, and R. S. SCHIAVO (1971) "Data feedback: a rationale," in H. A. Hornstein et al., Social Intervention: A Behavioral Science Approach. New York: Free Press.

MILES, M. -B. and D. G. LAKE (1967) "Self-renewal in school systems: a strategy for planned change," in G. Watson (ed.) Concepts for Social Change. Washington, D.C.: NEA.

MINTZ, E. (1971) "Marathon groups: process and people," in L. Blank et al., Confrontation. New York: Macmillan.

PATTERSON, C. H. (1973) Theories of Counseling and Psychotherapy. New York: Harper & Row.

SCHEIN, E. H. (1969) Process Consultation: Its Role in Organization Development. Reading, Mass.: Addison-Wesley.

SCHMUCK, R. A. and M. B. MILES [eds.] (1971) Organization Development in Schools. Palo Alto, Calif.: National Press Books.

SCHMUCK, R. A., P. RUNKEL, and D. LANGMEYER (1971) "Using group problem-solving procedures," in R. A. Schmuck and M. B. Miles (eds.) Organization Development in Schools. Palo Alto, Calif.: National Press Books.

WOLPE, J. (1968) "Some methods of behavior therapy," in C. E. Walker et al., Behavior Theory and Therapy. State of California Department of Mental Hygiene Research Symposium 2.

——— (1958) Psychotherapy by Reciprocal Inhibition. Stanford: Stanford Univ. Press.

WOLPIN, M. (1968) "Guided imagining in reducing fear and avoidance behavior," in C. E. Walker et al., Behavior Theory and Therapy. State of California Department of Mental Hygiene Research Symposium 2.

# BRINGING PARENTS AND STUDENTS INTO SCHOOL MANAGEMENT
## A New Program of Research and Development on Organization Development

RICHARD A. SCHMUCK
*Center for Educational Policy and Management and*
*Department of Educational Psychology*
*University of Oregon*

**When Matt Miles and I** carried out an extensive international search for OD interventions in schools back in 1970, we did not come up with any projects in which parents, students, and educators were being simultaneously involved. Of the handful of school OD projects that we did find (Schmuck and Miles, 1971), virtually every practitioner defined the professional staff as being synonymous with the school organization. Students and parents were not included. It was true that the Educational Change Team (Chesler and Lohman, 1971) was attempting to engage students with educators, that the Mott Community schools were striving to put parents and teachers into better communication, and that Phil Runkel and I were pilot-testing an OD training program involving parents and educators; nevertheless, there was no project of an OD sort that was bringing parents, students, and educators together for planned organizational change.

---

AUTHOR'S NOTE: *Many of the ideas in this paper were developed jointly with Dr. Philip J. Runkel.*

Now, in 1973, we at Oregon have set out to remedy this situation. Phil Runkel and I have put together a tentative plan for a research and development program that we are currently calling, "Strategies for Bringing Parents, Students, and Educators Into Joint Decision Making." The problem this program will attack is the gap between the generally ineffective and sporadic way that parents and students presently share in educational decisions and a well-organized procedure through which parents and students can make decisions with educators. We plan to adapt the methods of organization development to build organizational structures through which parents, students, and educators can, much more easily and effectively than is now typical, enter into collaborative decision-making about educational matters. This paper describes some of the thinking and prior research that has gone into the development of this embryonic program.

## INTERVENTION STRATEGY OF THE PROGRAM

The strategy we propose for bringing parents and students into school management is essentially one that alters interpersonal norms, builds new subsystems within or beside the school organization, and eventually produces a flexible, problem-solving or self-renewing school community. It is a strategy that seeks its effects by altering the relationships between individuals, particularly in terms of interpersonal norms and skills, not the psychological characteristics of the individuals themselves. Moreover, the strategy assumes that modifications in organizational structures—especially structural changes that involve the inclusion of heretofore neglected participants such as parents and students—do not become stable without concomitant changes in interpersonal norms and skills.

We have self-consciously discarded psychodynamic strategies that seek to improve organizational functioning by improving the capabilities of individuals. Thus, we have decided against training principals or teachers to be more skillful in dealing with parents or students. Likewise, we have decided against giving special training to parents or students in how to confront and communicate with school people. And, at the other side of thinking about social interventions, we have discarded the strategy of fiat—of directing the organization to change form without educating participants in new norms and skills. Thus, we also have discarded the plan of inserting a new position into a school district for "improving community relations," or the idea of a number of new committees and ad hoc task-groups of parents, students, and educators to evaluate and make plans for change.

We conceive the problem of this program as essentially social psychological. Our OD approach changes the social structure through modifying the interpersonal communication patterns among parents, students, and educators. It alters the norms that shape the potentialities for collaboration among parents, students, and educators. We believe that a successful strategy acts directly on the interpersonal agreements about permissible, prohibited, and desirable kinds of interpersonal actions. Such a strategy educates intact groups to practice the new norms. The individual parents, students, and educators must be able, first, to conceive new ways of acting, but then, also, the actual individuals who will be interacting in the new relationships must practice together to use the new norms in solving their own actual problems.

## THEORY AND TECHNOLOGY OF OD—OREGON STYLE

For the past six years, Phil Runkel and I have been developing a theory and technology of OD in schools. The results of our efforts have been elaborated in Schmuck and Runkel (1972, 1970); Schmuck et al. (1971); Langmeyer et al. (1971); Schmuck and Miles (1971); and Schmuck et al. (1972). Here I wish to summarize some of the most salient points.

The theory we have been developing can be divided into

static and dynamic parts. The static side contains these postulates:

First, school organizations are complex social systems that are made up of subsystems within the customary meanings of general systems theory. Subsystems are stabilized primarily by norms having to do with role reciprocations. We use the term *role reciprocations* to emphasize the fact that roles do not reside within individuals nor in individual positions; roles lie *between* persons or jobs. Organizations act through communicative networks; these are also events between persons. Where proper norms and skills do not exist for effective communicative links, action cannot be transmitted from one part of the organization to another.

Second, the motives most salient in organizational life are *achievement, power,* and *affiliation.* Although all individuals partake of all three, each person favors one over the others in given situations and from time to time.

Third, most often persons seek satisfactions at work that are constructive for the organization. They do not seek satisfactions such as those available from sabotage or goldbricking unless other satisfactions such as constructive achievement, camaraderie, or mastery are closed to them.

The dynamic part of the theory can be summarized with the following postulates:

First, a school's goals always are in flux. The satisfaction and frustration an individual experiences in relation to organizational goals are also always in flux. The direction of an individual's own goals alter as the nature of his participation in the organization shifts. The task accomplishment of a school is some compound of its formal goals, the individual goals of the persons within it, and the goals of the persons and organizations in its environment.

Second, there is a character of human subsystems known variously as morale, esprit de corps, synergy, or charisma. Improving this aspect of a school's climate can accelerate change and strengthen the momentum of change.

Third, educators, parents, and students will acquire new

patterns of behavior not only by visualizing them, but also by directly modeling the behaviors of their coparticipants. Consequently, training groups to produce new norms and to put new skills into action will gain strength from practicing the new behaviors within the intact groups and moving in stages from the old way to the new by practicing each shifted pattern with coparticipants.

Fourth, learning new role reciprocations can proceed most rapidly by enabling the individuals to act with coparticipants in the new way first, and afterward to fit a cognitive framework around the acts. Subsequently, the newly acquired cognitive framework makes the acts easier to perform in other circumstances.

Fifth, newly formed groups of educators, parents, and students must necessarily proceed through several stages of development before they become smoothly productive. These stages will include settling the issues of trust, closeness, and influence patterns within the group. As the group's relation to the community environment changes, the exact tasks of the group will change, and these former stages will have to be recycled.

The technology of organization development that we have generated at Oregon is featured by experiential learning and is constituted of skill training, group and intergroup exercises, data survey feedback, and innovative group procedures. Concerning skill training, participants are given opportunities to practice various activities in communication, problem-solving, and decision-making in an open and supportive climate. This "safe" atmosphere increases the ease of trying out new behaviors and of risking new ideas and feelings. While some of the skills are introduced through lecturettes and readings, the important learning comes when the group practices the skills in exercises or simulations, and while it works on its own issues and problems. As group members become more skillful and competent in group processes and interpersonal skills, group trust develops. As the group learns that its members are competent and motivated to help the group, it becomes easier to make contributions that are helpful rather than unhelpful or harmful to the group's processes.

Exercises may illuminate processes either within or between groups. Through some exercises (or simulations), group members interact with one another, while focusing on a specific aspect of the way they work together. In these "learning games," participants study communication, problem-solving, and decision-making without the pressures that build up in their real jobs. A group might work together solving a puzzle, then discuss learnings about cooperation, and finally look at ways of being more cooperative in planning a new program.

An important technique used in an organization development intervention is called data survey feedback. The group learns to generate important and valid data about itself by asking each person (survey) to share his or her impressions and feelings (data) about the way the group works. All this information is collected and combined into a single picture of what the group is thinking and feeling. The picture is reported (feedback) to the group and publically considered to serve as a springboard for planning and action. This technique is useful when the group is setting goals, solving problems, making decisions, implementing proposals, or assessing movement toward stated goals.

As part of OD interventions, participants are also taught several new procedures that lead to increased group effectiveness. Procedures differ from exercises in that they are methods of operating that a group can use repeatedly in its daily work. For example, a particular goal identification procedure may help the group more effectively define its problems. The use of the "fishbowl" procedure may increase meeting effectiveness by involving more group members in discussions and decisions. A structured activity may help group members uncover conflicts so that they can be managed in constructive ways. These and the other techniques of OD are described in Schmuck et al. (1972).

## SPECIAL CHALLENGES THIS PROGRAM FACES

Past attempts to involve students and parents in generating educational alternatives have had few productive outcomes. The scarcity of successes has been at least partly due to the failure of teachers and administrators to relinquish sufficient control so that the power of students and parents could be constructively increased. A recent study by Chesler (1973) pointed to a few of the barriers to effective student participation in school governance. She listed the students' prior socialization to depend on adult authorities; the students' lack of political skills, and the creation by the adult professionals of school structures and processes most comfortable for adults and thus easier to dominate. Even though Chesler was focusing on students, we believe similar barriers would apply to parent participation. Their prior socialization to depend on educated experts, their lack of political organization and know-how, and their inability to penetrate the school structure would keep parents from effectively collaborating with educators in school management.

Lack of collaboration among parents, students, and educators also has been due to the absence of norms and skills on the part of all three groups for problem-solving and decision-making. Most student-government councils have had little opportunity to participate in formulating policy on important school issues and lack the skill for interacting effectively with the faculty. Most PTAs are powerless and ineffective for similar reasons. Since the problem lies primarily in the ways that educators, parents, and students interact, we believe that only new norms for interpersonal problem-solving and new organizational structures for communication and decision-making among the three groups will be effective. The traditional norms of "professional autonomy," "educational elitism," and "ageism" must be replaced by shared expectations in support of collaboration among all involved parties, respect for expertness, and tolerance for intergenerational differences. These traditional norms will not be changed easily, but we believe they must change for true collaboration to occur among parents, students, and educators.

We face other sorts of challenges besides these. Probabilities are that the OD consultation will be considerably more complicated logistically than it was when we were working only with educators. For example, the matter of times and places for training and meetings will be much more complicated when we work with parents and students. Indeed, the logistical arrangements of training sessions will be further complicated as we work with lower-class parents and elementary-age students. The very poorest parents, of course, will be difficult to reach and to get to our meetings, while young students (and hard-working parents) may not have the energy to meet with educators and trainers during the evenings. We will also face such challenges in working with lower-class parents and young students as the lack of a common and easily understandable language, the lack of sufficient trust and rapport, and the lack of sufficient optimism about the possibilities of joint work with educators leading to much real change.

Above all, the major challenge this program faces is to find ways of bringing educators, parents, and students more often within the same cycle of decision-making. Currently these three bodies each have some degree of influence on the school, but usually not in the same cycle. The predominant body, the educators, is made up of administrators and teachers. Administrators typically make a decision and take action to put it into effect; the teachers, students, and parents then react to the administrators' actions. Reactions of the teachers may come a few weeks after the first administrative decision, while reactions of students and parents occur later. Administrators then react to these reactions and another sequence of cycles begins. The organizational structure that we hope to help create would bring influence from all four groups to bear upon appropriate decisions before any full-scale effort to carry out the decision is set in motion. In other words, all segments—the administrators, teachers, parents, and students—would have influence upon the decision, share in some way in converting the decision into action, and react, more or less simultaneously, to the effects of the decision they shared in making.

Of course, all four segments of the school will not participate in every educational decision; such complete democracy would be virtually impossible and very inefficient. Indeed, one of the important tasks of this new program will be to ascertain criteria for assigning some decisions to all four segments and others to one, two, or three of the segments. We believe that a variety of decision-making structures are conceivable that could support a norm for collaborative problem-solving among administrators, teachers, parents, and students, and that it will be our task to test some of the combinations of these structures.

## PILOT STUDIES

Although our research and development on involving students in school OD projects have been very meager, we have used survey data from high school students to induce problem-solving in teachers and administrators (Flynn, 1971); evaluated the effects of OD consultation on classroom group processes in a junior high school (Bigelow, 1971); and worked with fifth and sixth graders in one OD project to help them come together with their teachers into productive problem-solving (Schmuck, 1973). Beyond these minor involvements in working with students and educators in OD, two pilot efforts constitute the primary backdrop for our new program. Presently, we are launching an OD project with parents, students, and educators of an intermediate school in an urban district on the West Coast. And, in one recently completed project, we did explore—in some detail—the use of OD methods to bring parents and educators into joint problem-solving. I will discuss this latter project first.

## PARENTS AND EDUCATORS

From November 1971 to October 1972, we were involved with most of the parents and all of the teachers and administrators of the Thomas Elementary School (pseudonym) in an urban school district on the West Coast. The principal sought consultative help after receiving a lengthy memo from parents on the weaknesses of the Thomas program. Our consultative team agreed to provide OD training for both the parents and the staff separately and then later to provide consultation that would help the two groups to come together into effective collaboration. Our consultative team planned to focus on issues related to improving communication within and between the two groups, to improving the openness and supportiveness between the groups, and to increasing the amount and quality of the two groups' collaborative problem-solving. Our initial objectives were: (1) to open and clarify communication between the parents and the staff; (2) to bring parents and staff together into collaborative problem-solving; and (3) to provide OD training and consultation for the staff during and after the parent-staff problem-solving.

Having determined some objectives and the sort of intervention that could be made, we developed a macro design for the OD consultation which was aimed at spanning a period of about one calendar year. We decided to incorporate a variety of intervention modes in the design, including training in communication skills and problem-solving, data feedback, confrontation, process consultation, and plan-making. In a meeting of a staff-parent steering committee for the project, this design was considered and approved. The macro design called for six stages:

*Stage 1.* Meet with the Thomas staff, an ad hoc parents' advisory group, and the project steering committee to explain the role, services, and methods of the consultants and to get each group to determine its willingness to take part in a demonstration meeting on organization development.

*Stage 2.* Provide demonstrations of OD to the staff and to interested parents in which the details of a plan to bring school and community together into collaborative problem-solving could be explained and during which the commitment of both groups to an extended intervention could be obtained. An audio-slide presentation developed by Arends, Phelps, Harris, and Schmuck (1973) on OD in schools was used at each of the demonstration sessions. Also, introductory booklets on OD in schools by Arends, Phelps, and Schmuck (1973) were made available to the Thomas staff and parents.

*Stage 3.* Train parents and staff separately in the skills of interpersonal communication and group processes, while at the same time helping each body to identify some issues of concern in relation to the Thomas program. Participants were asked to describe those behaviors on the part of staff and parents that were helpful or not in building an effective program at Thomas. They were also asked to paraphrase what others were saying, to describe their own feelings about facets of the school program, and to check the validity of their impressions of others' feelings.

*Stage 4.* Bring the two bodies together to interact and to share perceptions each had of the other, to identify areas where each body was viewed as helpful or unhelpful to the other, to establish clear communication channels between the two groups, to introduce a problem-solving procedure that would facilitate collaborative inquiry into mutual problems, and to identify the common concerns that the total community wished to work on. The "Imaging Exercise" described by Schmuck et al. (1972: 158-159) was employed during this stage with sixty parents and all Thomas staff members in a marathon evening session lasting seven hours.

*Stage 5.* Form special task groups composed of both staff and parents which would select one or two of the identified concerns and participate in collaborative problem-solving. Problem-solving procedures discussed in Schmuck et al. (1972: 220-254) were used during this stage.

*Stage 6.* Finally, bring all participants together to share the results of these problem-solving activities and to make decisions and plans for implementation.

In an extensive, detailed technical report on the Thomas project, Phelps and Arends (1973) discussed the historical background behind this macro design, the details of its implementation, and the eventual outcomes of the intervention. Before summarizing some of those outcomes, I wish to underscore some of the key features of the intervention because they will be instructive for future efforts to involve parents, students, and educators in OD projects.

First, making careful and prolonged entry was very important. Indeed, the entry process with the parents and staff of Thomas School required an intensive two months of effort on our parts. This was because we faced some logistical problems—parents could only meet in the evenings and the staff was most available right after school. Moreover, the usual channels for contacting a wide variety of parents about special meetings—sending memos home with the children— was not very reliable. In addition, organization development was a new concept for most of the parents and the staff. And obviously, there was a significant need to raise the parents' and teachers' levels of trust in us. There seemed to be some hesitation on the part of some staff members to becoming involved in training that would take time from other duties. Some parents seemed to hesitate in accepting the consultants' recommendations that they postpone confrontation until after a period of initial skill training in separate groups. Finally, we consultants ourselves were cognizant of the fact that this intervention was risky. Our skills, theory, and technology had not been tested previously with parent-staff groups, and yet success in this well-known school was important if OD was to continue to flourish in the district.

A second key point of the design was separating parents and staff for the initial training. This decision was based primarily on our belief that it would be necessary to provide preliminary help to the staff which was under attack and outnumbered by the parents (at one point, sixteen staff members faced ninety parents). The Thomas staff lacked a sense of efficacy or potency in relation to a confrontation with parents. Furthermore, neither the staff nor this collection of parents had spent time in their separate groups to set goals or to develop themselves into more than a collection of individuals.

At the same time, while the two groups were separated for initial training events, specific plans were made for reducing the social distance which such a strategy might have created between the parents and the staff. First, all consultants tried to avoid becoming identified as belonging to one group or the other by working with both groups at different times. And second, the ad hoc steering committee was composed of parents and staff members who continued to meet regularly throughout the intervention period, serving as a group where information about what was happening or should happen with the parent and staff groups was shared and discussed.

A third key point of the design was that of improving interpersonal skills and group procedures of the two bodies in the context of problem identification and diagnosis. There were several reasons for amalgamating skill training and diagnosis during the first three stages of our macro design. First, since the parents and staff seemed to be task-centered and very serious, we decided to use the actual problems the two groups saw as content for initial discussions. (Often our OD designs have introduced skills through simulations.) Second, this strategy made it possible to separate in a clear fashion the steps of problem identification, solution generation, and decision-making for innovative actions. Maier (1970) has shown that such a trichotomy is important for achieving solutions of high quality and internalized acceptance. Third, because the staff lacked the time and parents seemed to lack the patience to undergo extensive training, procedures that facilitate communication in large groups (fishbowls, surveys, and recording on newsprint) were incorporated directly into the activities for problem identification rather than being taught and practiced as separate training activities.

Some of the outcomes of the OD consultation for the parents and educators at Thomas school were: (1) A committee of parents and staff worked during the summer to draft a revised constitution and bylaws for the PTA which included parents participating in goal-setting, rule-setting, and curriculum evaluation. The new organization has become a going concern; election of officers for 1973-1974 has been held and continuation of the new participative structures seems likely. (2) A handbook containing information about school district policies, the administrative structure, school regulations, procedures, and programs and the newly structured PTA, was prepared and disseminated widely by a parent-staff subgroup. (3) Another subgroup of staff and parents proposed and implemented several projects to renovate, remodel, and generally improve various aspects of the school plant. (4) A new organization of parent volunteers for teaching and tutoring was developed and implemented. (5) An "artist-in-residence program" was organized and managed by a parent subgroup.

A year later, the parents were queried about their reactions to changes at Thomas school. While one-fifth of the parents qualified their statements in some way by commenting that the changes were not as extensive as they had hoped, all parents who were interviewed identified some improvements at the school. About three-fifths of the parents mentioned their involvement in one of the five outcomes listed above, while four-fifths reported general improvements in the quality of relationships between staff and parents. The parents' reactions to the new handbook and a new newsletter were uniformly enthusiastic, and the new format and character of the PTA appealed to most parents, because of more satisfying and stimulating opportunities for the exchange of information with the staff.

Furthermore, according to data from 1973 interviews, the staff had clearly become much more receptive to having parents involved in more activities in the school. Sixty-two percent of the staff described working conditions with fellow staff members as "better," while the other 38% rated the situation as "about the same." Those who saw improvements attributed these to the fact of better parent-staff relationships. The parents—at the same time—perceived an increase in their own actual influence and did so without perceiving a decrease in the influence of the teachers. Both the parents and teachers saw the PTA as being a key context in which everybody's influence was being increased. Many more details have been described in Phelps and Arends (1973).

## PARENTS, STUDENTS, AND EDUCATORS

At present, we are beginning the very first stages of an OD consultation with parents, students, and educators of an intermediate school (grades 7 and 8) in an urban district on the West Coast. The present, very sketchy, macro design for the experimental intervention has four phases after entry: (1) train each body in communication skills, establishing objectives, uncovering and working on conflicts, conducting meetings, solving problems in groups, and collecting data; (2) bring the three bodies together to explore goals, uncover differences, and agree upon problems that stand in the way of joint decision-making and other uses of human resources; (3) let small heterogeneous problem-solving groups (with students, parents, and educators as members) work collaboratively on problems identified during stage 2; and (4) build some new structural arrangements out of the multiple realities shared during stages 2 and 3 and as part of the solution of problems worked out during stage 3.

Some typical questions that we will be trying to answer as we move along are: With which body (parents, students, or educators) should we spend most time in the beginning? How do we achieve representation among the parents? What are the sorts of conflicts between black and white, male and female, and the social classes that will affect the first steps in accelerating communication? How do we open communication and develop rapport among students across differences of skill, values, age, race, social class, and sex? Will we be able to maintain a multipartisan stance in relation to all three bodies? How do we keep the students from becoming pawns in battles between the teachers and parents? How will we assess readiness for confrontation? These and many other question lay before us.

## CONCLUSION

In whatever ways these questions are answered, we are confident that the benefits of a new organizational arrangement to facilitate joint decision-making among administrators, teachers, parents, and students will be of at least three types. First, the sheer disruption and waste of unwarranted conflict will be reduced, while the educational issues underlying the conflicts will be made clearer. Second, new procedures will become available to facilitate proposed changes in educational methods that rest on the collaboration of the four groups. And third, new resources in all four bodies will be discovered, shared, and used. We predict that the new awareness about how to use different resources will result in changed relations within classrooms; these changed interactions between teachers and students, in turn, will lead to greater attractiveness between teachers and students, reduced absenteeism on the part of both, and an acceleration in the use of participative classroom methods. If these improved relations persist for several years, we further predict that the collaborative organizational arrangement will result in the schools becoming self-renewing organizations, rearranging their goals and procedures to cope with changes in the environment.

# REFERENCES

ARENDS, R., J. PHELPS, M. HARRIS, and R. A. SCHMUCK (1973) Organization Development in Schools. Eugene, Oregon: Center for Educational Policy and Management. (an audio-slide presentation)

ARENDS, R., J. PHELPS, and R. A. SCHMUCK (1973) Organization Development: Building Human Systems in Schools. Eugene, Oregon: Center for Educational Policy and Management.

BIGELOW, R. (1971) "Changing classroom interaction through organization development," pp. 71-85 in R. A. Schmuck and M. B. Miles (eds.) Organization Development in Schools. Palo Alto, Calif.: National Press Books.

CHESLER, J. (1973) "Innovative governance structures in secondary schools." J. of Applied Behavioral Sci. 9, 2/3: 261-280.

——— and J. LOHMAN (1971) "Changing schools through student advocacy," pp. 185-212 in R. A. Schmuck and M. B. Miles (eds.) Organization Development in Schools. Palo Alto, Calif.: National Press Books.

FLYNN, W. (1971) The Principal as an Organizational Consultant to His Own School. Ph.D. dissertation. University of Oregon.

LANGMEYER, D., R. A. SCHMUCK, and P. J. RUNKEL (1971) "Technology for organizational training in schools." Soc. Inquiry 41, 2: 193-204.

MAIER, N.R.F. (1970) Problem Solving and Creativity in Individuals and Groups. Belmont, Calif.: Brooks-Cole.

PHELPS, J. and R. ARENDS (1973) "Helping parents and educators to solve school problems together: an application of organization development." Eugene, Oregon: Center for Educational Policy and Management Technical Report.

SCHMUCK, R. A. (1973) "Group dynamics and classroom behavior," pp. 245-263 in CRM Books (eds.) Educational Psychology: A Contemporary View. Del Mar, Calif.

——— and M. B. MILES (1971) Organization Development in Schools. Palo Alto, Calif.: National Press Books.

SCHMUCK, R. A. and P. J. RUNKEL (1972) "Integrating organizational specialists into school districts," pp. 168-200 in W. W. Burke (ed.) Contemporary Organization Development: Conceptual Orientations and Interventions. Washington, D.C.: NTL Institute for Applied Behavioral Science.

——— (1970) Organizational Training for a School Faculty. Eugene, Oregon: Center for Educational Policy and Management.

——— and D. LANGMEYER (1970) "Theory to guide organizational training in schools." Soc. Inquiry 41, 2: 183-191.

SCHMUCK, R. A., P. J. RUNKEL, S. SATUREN, R. MARTELL, and C. B. DERR (1972) Handbook of Organization Development in Schools. Palo Alto, Calif.: National Press Books.

# AN INNER-CITY SCHOOL THAT CHANGED—AND CONTINUED TO CHANGE

ARTHUR BLUMBERG
*School of Education*
*Syracuse University*

JAMES MAY
*Dr. Martin Luther King Elementary School*
*Syracuse, New York*

ROGER PERRY
*School of Education*
*Syracuse University*

An observant "over-forty" visitor to most public schools today will be struck by the singular fact that what goes on in them is markedly similar to what transpired in the schools he attended as a youngster. This is not to say that math or science, for example, are not being taught differently (for better or for worse) in some cases. Nor is it to suggest that new courses with attractive and "relevant" titles have not been introduced into the curriculum (again, for better or for worse). But it is to take note of the fact that, for the most part, the basic structure of the school, the way decisions are made, the character of the relationships between administrators and teachers, teachers and teachers, and teachers and students, tend to be what they used to be. And this despite the fact that large sums of money and astronomical numbers of person hours have been devoted to trying to induce change in the schools so that they might become more responsive and open social systems.

This article describes an exception to this "change but no change" (Sarason, 1971) phenomenon. It considers the case of an inner-city school (Dr. Martin Luther King Elementary School, Syracuse, N.Y.) that changed, initially by restructuring its decision-making processes, and continued to change to meet new community and educational problems.

In an earlier paper, Blumberg et al. (1969) described the thinking and activities that accompanied the change in the decision-making structure of King School when a new principal was appointed (the principal had taken a leave from his university professorship in order to go "where the action was"). The change involved a shift in the decision-making pattern from one that was hierarchical (principal makes the decisions) to a participative one (teachers and principal collaborate on decision-making). What was discussed in that article was a matter-of-fact description and analysis of events concerning the change and its effects. It contained no theoretical rationale for the restructuring; its goal, rather simply, was to say, "this was what happened."

In the present paper, we revisit the school for a look at what evolved from that participative decision-making structure change. Our concerns are two: first, to inquire, broadly, into the effects that the change had on the life of teachers in the school. The second is to illustrate how the new structure resulted in (1) the ability of the teachers to develop and use power, (2) an ingathering of school parents into the decision-making structure and their use of power, and (3) a switch from teacher focus on broad policy-making to a participative concern with instructional improvement.

## SOME EFFECTS OF THE CHANGE ON TEACHERS

In retrospect, the newly appointed principal's move to alter the decision-making pattern was based on the notion that the structural properties of the school fall legitimately within a principal's prerogative to control and, therefore, change. The point is that, contrary to public pronouncements, principals, for the most, have little direct control over curriculum matters or teachers' classroom behavior. What the principal clearly has control of is the formal structural arrangement of the school by which, for example, faculty are communicated with and decisions are made.

So it was, perhaps through some implicit sensing of the parameters of his power, that the principal's early action was focused on altering the decision-making sturcture of the school. There was no long, drawn-out debate about it. It was—simply—done, and King school found itself with a decision-making group known as the cabinet, composed of elected teacher representatives and three administrators, each of whom had one vote.

Changes in one part of a social system have consequences for other parts. So it was with King School. In particular, there were consequences for those parts of school life that involved adults relating with adults. Issues of technical change (i.e., problems of teaching style and curriculum) were less immediately affected by the change in decision-making style.

Thus, though the opportunity to make policy decisions about the school was greeted enthusiastically by most of the teachers, the actual operation of the system engendered some new and unsettling factors into the organizational life of the school. Most importantly, these were:

(1) The teachers became frustrated with themselves because they found they were relatively inept in group problem-solving and decision-making skills.

(2) The teachers became unsure and insecure about the limits of their power. They did not know whether or not to trust the principal.

(3) The stability that accompanies a traditional principal-teacher relationship was greatly reduced.

## LACK OF GROUP PROBLEM-SOLVING SKILLS

What became immediately apparent, as teachers were elected and met as the decision-making body of the school, was that they were ill-equipped, behaviorally, to function as a group. This fact had little to do with personalities and more to do with the kind of organizational role for which they were trained and which, for the most part, teachers are still being trained today. That is, the organizational role for which teachers are prepared is almost exclusively focused on the teacher-pupil relationship. Both the content and skill training of preservice teacher education are concerned with teaching qua teaching. Practically none of their energy is concerned with learning about the school as a human organization or learning how to function as an adult peer in that organization. It may be that the implicit assumptions behind this lack of concern with helping teachers learn roles other than their "teacher" one are that (1) the kind of adult-adult relationships that a teacher has in a school are relatively unimportant when measured against classroom life, and (2) the kinds of skills necessary to function with adults collaboratively are easy to come by.

In situations such as that which we are describing, it turns out that if either or both of these assumptions are made the results are likely to be unfortunate. In specific, for example, it developed that adult-adult relationships became relatively more salient to the teachers in the school even though the major part of their day was devoted to youngsters. It also developed that they were quite unskilled in group problem-solving. But how could it be otherwise? Their jobs had never previously demanded that they work and devote energy to each other in more than a "ships passing in the night" way.

## THE QUESTION OF TEACHER POWER

The very crucial factor of the extent of teacher power entered the situation. The questions implicitly asked by teachers in meeting after meeting was, "Is this a game we are playing or is it for real? Do we really have the power to run the school or is it a facade whereby our skillful new principal gets us to arrive at decisions he wants but also gets us to think the decisions were ours?"

The teachers could scarcely be blamed for being skeptical about the power issue. Their training and experience had run counter to the notion that decision-making power could be shared by principal and teachers in any meaningful kind of way. In addition, though the idea of having the power to make meaningful decisions is an attractive one, the culture of the schools clearly seems to have developed a norm among many teachers that suggests, "he gets paid for making decisions. We get paid for teaching. Leave us out of it." At King School there were teachers who felt so strongly about this that they refused to take part in the process.

## LOSS OF STABILITY

A third and unpredicted factor that derived from moving the school into a participative decision-making mode was the unsettling effect on the stability of the organization. King is an inner-city school that was committed to move from a custodial "keep-things-cool" orientation to one devoted to helping children learn and grow. The program changes that were introduced and the efforts to get teachers to be more responsible problem solvers, had sometimes ended in chaos. And to make matters worse, by going to a participative structure the principal had, in effect, told the teachers that he would help them, but in the final analysis, they had to deal with the problems and make the decisions.

By hindsight, it seems conceptually clear (at the time it was fuzzy) that if the changed structure was to take hold and become an integrated and valued facet of school life, attention would have to be given to working on these problems or the new structure would collapse. And the collapse would be accompanied by great disillusion. The bottom would have dropped out. Guided more by intuition than theory, several positions were taken by the principal in order to avoid this potential disintegration. These were:

(1) It would be necessary to intervene, either through ongoing activities or inservice training, in order to help the teachers learn and become skillful at group problem-solving and decision-making.

(2) Every opportunity would have to be taken to encourage and reinforce the assumption of power by teachers.

(3) The principal would have continually to refuse to be seduced into "taking charge" so that the system could develop its own peer-level source of stability.

(4) There would have to be a continual monitoring of the system so that organizational problems could be confronted and dealt with quickly rather than letting them fester below the surface.

These positions did not take the form of school policy. Rather, they became operational through various programmatic and personal efforts. For example:

— The agenda of each cabinet meeting included time for a process analysis of what had occurred during the meeting so that teachers could start to develop their own internal feedback system.

— Inservice workshops were devoted to group dynamics and problem-solving skills in which the entire faculty was involved.

— A six-week summer institute for faculty on curriculum development included a week of sensitivity training.

— One inservice afternoon was given over entirely to clarifying principal-teacher role expectations through a confrontation design (Golembiewski and Blumberg, 1968).

— The principal continually refused to deal personally with a teacher who had an organizationally related problem. The teacher and the problem were referred to the cabinet.

The focus of these efforts was to create, not an all-loving, peaceful school, but a new type of organization in which, or so it was hoped, (1) teachers would gain a new kind of respect for each other as adults, and (2) a climate would develop that could serve as a base through which teachers could exercise power intelligently and the parents could be brought into the scene in a productive fashion. But these are very general goals. They are the type of goals, in fact, that plague the field of education because of their very generality. More specificity is required. And so, in our second look at King School, our aim was to uncover case data that might shed light on the following questions which, though still relatively broad, provide a somewhat sounder base for analyzing results than the goal statements. These questions were:

(1) Is King School more of an open system with renewal characteristics now than it was several years ago? Does it consider new ideas and does it import new energy into itself?

(2) Has participative decision-making taken root in the organization or is it merely a structural change that exists on paper?

(3) Has the organization over time developed stability so that it can deal effectively with itself and its environment—i.e., external pressures?

(4) In what ways has the initial change intervention affected more than just the structure? That is, in Leavitt's (1965) terms how have the human relations and technological segments of the organization been altered by the structural change?

The next section of this paper presents some case vignettes that shed light on these questions. The vignettes, of course, are not in the category of hard, quantitative data, but for our purposes hard data are not the issue. The vignettes provide a rich flavor of the school and its climate. They describe what happened in the school as it confronted, with its new structure, four separate but related issues. These were: (1)

the selection of a new principal, (2) the development of parent-influence on the school's decision-making structure, (3) the stabilizing of the organization, and (4) problems of technological (curriculum) change.

## THE SELECTION OF A NEW PRINCIPAL

The principal who initiated the change effort resigned to take a university position three years after the original intervention. The teachers wanted direct participation in the reelection process while the central office wanted to exclude them. This issue is significant because it caused a power struggle between the school's teachers and part of the central office staff.

The essence of the confrontation revolved around control. In many ways the original principal was not responsible to the central office and acted accordingly. He was paid by the university and had been immune to typical central office pressures. Obviously, many central office people resented this freedom and felt a principal more malleable to their values was needed.

The teachers' stand was quite different. Over the past few years they had worked on developing the skills of participative decision-making and they placed a high value on the way their school was run. The principal was morally bound to carry out their decisions. The teachers had personally invested heavily in this structure and wanted to retain it. They realized the selection of the principal was crucial.

Unless the new principal supported the cabinet notion, all the gains the teachers had made in the past three years would have been in jeopardy. They felt that the perpetuation of their organizational structure was at stake. Therefore, the cabinet (i.e., teachers) decided to act affirmatively to gain the right to enter the selection process. Political power was generated to apply pressure on the central office. This was accomplished by holding several staff meetings after school, by having meetings with parents, and by an exhaustive series of telephone calls. This well-organized effort could not go unheard. The superintendent finally gave the cabinet the right to be involved in the process. They became active in both interviewing candidates and making recommendations to the superintendent. This process was not a perfunctory one. Even though the cabinet's and parents' choice was not acceptable to many central office personnel, he was appointed principal. And, it is interesting to note that, apparently cueing on this incident, other faculties in the system have asserted themselves similarly when new principals were appointed to their school.

## THE DEVELOPMENT OF PARENT INFLUENCE ON DECISION-MAKING

The substantive issues around which parent influence developed were: (1) what the goal of black education meant to the school, and (2) the reopening of a building closed by the board of education. It had been closed due to a clash between the positions of black administrators concerning black educational goals and the existing policies of the school district.

To get a better feeling for these issues, some background is necessary. The City of Syracuse at the time was facing the problems of integration, busing, and growing black awareness. The principal of the school, a young black man with black values, put forth his ideas by actively engaging in community programs in a city that was conservatively white and uptight. An inevitable clash occurred which almost shook the school apart. As an active member in community groups, the principal joined a group of concerned citizens who were attempting to elect black members to the board of education. After some frustrating defeats the group decided to get the public's attention dramatically by proposing that an all black board of education was needed for black students. Their strategy was to emphasize that the present board of education was all white and thirty percent of the kids in the school system were black.

The involvement of the principal in this announcement, which was in part a political ploy designed to involve parents in black education, caused much dissension within the staff and school community. Many parents were upset by this stance. They felt both they and the staff had worked hard for years to effect a successful model for voluntary integration. It is quite understandable that parents challenged the new principal who wanted to tear down their "progress."

The ploy worked. Meetings were held with parents to discuss what the principal and other black educators were trying to effect. The parents became very vocal in these well-attended meetings. After many of them, the parents and educators reached agreement on a redefinition of black education in the school. Nothing more has been heard about the black board of education.

As all this was going on, the school was reorganizing its decision-making process to include parents in its formal structure. The composition of the cabinet changed mainly from teachers to parents. Therefore, the parents had a legitimate organizational position to influence school policy. And that position had been achieved in the absence of confrontation politics.

After updating the school's goals, the parents were confronted with another problem. Several years ago the school board, in cooperation with the university, had established a school on the university campus that was an adjunct building to the main King building. It was known as King-on-Campus and its goal was to develop new programs for black youngsters. During the black school board turmoil, the board of education decided unilaterally to shut the doors of this building. The board's justification for this action was that the campus school had not been productive. However, community feeling was that the decision was politically motivated, an effort to get rid of the principal of that school who had been a thorn in the board's side. The new cabinet felt that the school's bylaws stated that King-on-Campus was under their jurisdiction and a unilateral decision was illegal. In addition, they considered King-on-Campus was an integral part of the King program and that they could not afford to lose this resource. Therefore, the cabinet challenged this decision.

After considerable discussion, the superintendent agreed that the cabinet could not be excluded from matters concerning King-on-Campus. This was the first time in Syracuse that parents had exerted enough influence to make decisions concerning their community education when it was in conflict with the board of education. Eventually, they offered a proposal to reopen King-on-Campus as a center that dealt with Afro-American studies. It was accepted. The center is still operating today under the control of the parent school.

## STABILIZING THE ORGANIZATION

The structure developed slowly following the original intervention. The cabinet originally gave teachers a mechanism to enter the decision-making process. In this phase the cabinet dealt with both long-range policy and short-range decisions concerning curriculum, discipline, scheduling, and the like. Over time, both the composition and function of the cabinet changed. As parents replaced teachers, the cabinet's focus became long range. The teachers formed an instructional improvement committee (IIC) that dealt with curriculum and everyday school management. Also, teams emerged to deal with different groups of students. Often the team leaders served on the IIC group. No formal structure held these groups together as the staff became more differentiated. Lines of communication and authority were fuzzy. A formal structure was needed to integrate these subgroups.

The Individually Guided Education (IGE) program which

was adopted in the fourth year of the participative pattern provided the needed format. IGE did not superimpose a new structure. Rather, it made explicit what already existed. It helped clarify the relationships and responsibilities among the groups and an interdependence among groups developed. The principal and cabinet became the legislative body. The IIC became a subcommittee of the cabinet and thus was able to link up with teaching teams.

There are two points to this particular vignette. First, stability in the school was established because IGE lent a formal instructional and curriculum pattern to the rather loose set of relationships that were in existence. Second, King School had been selected to experiment with IGE precisely because of its participative climate. It was a case of "goodness of fit."

These points are noted here less for their substance than to highlight the fact that all of these actions resulted from teacher concern and subsequent decision. What appears to have occurred, then, is that after several years of a "shake-down cruise," the system has changed substantially. While the values of the participative structure have been maintained, the participative energy and power of the teachers has been largely redirected from matters of broad policy to those of teaching and learning.

**TECHNOLOGICAL CHANGE**

The level of technological activity following the induction of the participative structure was low at first. However, in the past two years, much energy has been devoted to this area by teachers. Both parents and teachers have felt that the organization was now responsive to the community, that good human relations existed among parents, teachers, and students, and now the time was ripe for technological assessment and change. Since this shift in energy, much has happened.

Based on teacher decision, the school is now divided into

primary and intermediate levels. The reading program has been overhauled. At one time teachers could use the reading method they preferred. Now one approach is used by all teachers in the primary area. Also, learning policies were formed at the curriculum level. It was decided that there would be only one retention in seven years at King. This retention would take place at the primary grade. A third grade reading capability was the criteria. Also, youngsters are being continually reassessed, regrouped, and rescheduled in an effort to meet the individual needs of the students.

## SUMMARY

The vignettes provide some tentative answers to the questions that were raised earlier relative to whether the change to participative decision-making in King School was simply a matter of form or that it, indeed, was a change that made a difference. For example, there appears to be little doubt that the change intervention instituted a participative decision-making process functionally as well as structurally. Partial evidence for this is that teachers now have a strong say at the policy-making level, the everyday administrative level, and the curriculum level. Four teachers sit on the cabinet (long range). The IIC meets twice a week. One of the meetings concerns everyday administrative problems. The other deals with curriculum questions. Teachers have the responsibility to analyze curriculum programs, develop methods for evaluation, and make any programmatic changes with cabinet approval.

Bringing parents into the system was also more than a matter of form. For example, when the parents disagreed with the new principal on some of his black education goals they refused to rubber stamp his position. Rather, after considerable negotiations a joint resolution was reached that represented a set of mutual goals.

The question of renewal seems to be answered directly by the vignettes. The organization has been extremely adaptable to its changing environment. In a number of crises and planned efforts the system had changed both its philosophy and structure to meet new internal and external demands. Structurally this can be seen in the reorganization of the cabinet, in the implementation of IGE and the redefining of roles/responsibilities among teachers, parents, administrators, and the school board. In each case the organization sensed pressures from its environment, rallied resources for effective problem-solving, designed solutions, and successfully implemented these solutions. For example, the shift toward emphasis on black education was a major philosophical reorientation. The system successfully accepted the challenge and gained strength by working through these problems.

The development of a stable organization is another King characteristic. The school seemed to follow the classical process of differentiation and then integration through the development of interdependence among the differentiated parts. First the school differentiated itself by creating a cabinet to deal with short-run decisions and long-run policies and curriculum. The structure further differentiated when the cabinet's functions were split. Policy decisions remained with the reorganized cabinet while the short-run and curriculum decisions were the responsibility of the IIC. This group was further differentiated when one meeting a week was set for short-term decisions and one meeting for curriculum. The teams also represented further differentiation.

The formal integration process was brought about by IGE. This program explicated the relationship and responsibilities among these subgroups. It formalized the interdependence that had been developing. Differentiated subgroups were tied together into a definable organization structure that permitted the development of stability.

The structural intervention has also affected matters of human relations and technology. Teachers have learned to deal in an adult-to-adult manner with one another. More competence can be observed in the effective functioning of the cabinet, IIC, teams, and ad hoc committees. The level of communication, problem-solving, and decision-making skills has changed significantly over time. Norms related to these skills are now set firmly enough that both new teachers and parents become socialized to them just from being in the organization.

Although energy has been devoted to the technological area over the past six years, rapid change had not been evident until recently. This is mainly due to a shift of teacher focus from policy matters and human relations to instruction. Consequently, the IIC has spent its energy evaluating curriculum, spotting deficiencies, and implementing new programs. Decisions such as primary/intermediate divisions, a universal reading program, and only one retention in seven years illustrates some of the changes in the technological area.

## CONCLUSIONS

Clearly, it would be an error of the most gross proportion for the reader to have gotten the message from this paper that King School is an educational "land of milk and honey." Many problems and conflicts exist. The school has not solved the problem, for example, of making a serious and productive impact on the reading ability of inner-city black children, though some headway is being made. And, to an outside observer, walking into the school appears to be an experience in, at least, quasi-chaos. A colleague of ours, in this connection, commented that he could not get a feeling of who was in charge or what was its educational direction. But, perhaps, that was *his* problem.

In the last analysis, the developments at King, since it restructured itself, have been, we believe, relatively unique. The organizational decision-making model has survived in a sometimes hostile districtwide climate; the school worked through a change in principalship while maintaining its essential value system; and it expanded the concept of participative decision-making to include its parent community so that "community control" became more of a collaborative problem-solving issue than a political one. All this, of course, was not without problems and conflicts. But what apparently happened is that the original restructuring enabled the school organization to build a foundation through which it could maintain stability and continue to expand its renewal activities, both organizationally and programmatically. The school today resembles the school of six years ago, for the most part, only in its physical plant. What goes on inside it and between it and the community has changed and continues to do so. For example, a climate has developed that has enabled the school, as a human organization, to question and deal with previously unquestioned regularities of behavior and attitude (Sarason, 1971) that typically present barriers to the introduction and testing of new ideas. Reactions to innovative ideas, that is, tend to be, "if the idea has merit and can be tested, let's test it" rather than "we cannot do it because that is not the way it has been done" or "they will not let us." The school, then, though not an educational nirvana, is different enough so that a knowledgeable visitor to it commented recently that there was more going on there than in all the other elementary schools in the area combined.

One may not, of course, generalize with great confidence from an n = 1 study to a wide population. Nevertheless, based on our analysis of the King experience, we offer some propositions to schools, inner city or not, that may guide other schools as they seek to develop participative organizations that make a difference:

— The more abrupt the move to participative decision-making, the greater the unsettling effects on school organization life.

— The delegation of power to teachers will initially result in distrust of the principal.

— Unless attention is given to helping teachers learn collaborative skills the system will degenerate.

— When parents are involved in important problems they will respond with important energy.

Finally, the role of the principal in all this is not that of a pawn, to be moved about at the whim of his constituents. Our best concept of his role is that of a "hanging loose" leader who has an idea of where the school ought to go, who can both influence others and accept influence from them, and who sees his job as primarily involved with the creation of structures through which people can do their work most openly and freely.

## REFERENCES

BLUMBERG, A., W. WAYSON, and W. WEBER (1969) "The elementary school cabinet: report of an experience in participative decision making." Educ. Administrative Q. 5, 3: 33-52.

GOLEMBIEWSKI, R. T. and A. BLUMBERG (1968) "The laboratory approach to organization change: 'confrontation design.' " Academy of Management J. 11 (June): 199-210.

LEAVITT, H. J. (1965) "Applied organizational change in industry: structural technological and humanistic approaches," pp. 1144-1170 in J. G. March (ed.) Handbook of Organizations. Chicago: Rand McNally.

SARASON, S. (1971) The Culture of the School and the Problem of Change. Boston: Allyn & Bacon.

# CHUTZPA
## A Critical Review of the Preceding Papers

HARVEY A. HORNSTEIN
*Teachers College*
*Columbia University*

**Chutzpa is a Yiddish word** which is used to describe people or events that have a "quality of presumption plus arrogance." There is a sense in which the articles included in this publication have *chutzpa*.

During the past two decades, urban school systems have been beset by a number of stressful and traumatic events. Brutal and protracted racial confrontations have become almost commonplace; crime and narcotics abuse are rampant; the power of unions has multiplied and teacher's strikes are no longer uncommon; and, for sufficient and insufficient reasons, invective has been heaped upon school systems by students, parents, politicians and the press.

At the confluence of these events and so many others is the professional educator, battle-hardened and weary, simultaneously striving to survive and to keep the schools running. The merits and success of these efforts are matters for debate, but the recent struggles of professional educators are undeniable. They have been shot at, spit at, and shoved around.

Now it is 1973, and a group of papers about the applications of OD in urban school systems has been

[112]

prepared. Individually and collectively these papers talk about how the problems of urban school systems will be resolved through the use of meetings at which people diagnose their organization's condition and collaboratively plan and carry out remedial action. Ultimately, as a consequence of this process, organization structure will change, social norms will change, and some problems will move toward solution.

I believe that the authors' purposes in making these claims are sincere ones. I also believe that the weight of evidence is on their side and that their thrust is fundamentally correct. But, in the light of recent history, to assert that so few ordinary-sounding events can have such important effects, that is *chutzpa.*

The history and contemporary experience of organizations in any field of endeavor creates idiosyncratic effects which set them apart from other organizational groupings. Urban school systems are no exception. Although they contain dimensions which are common to all organizations, as Gabarro's article implies, they also have had a unique experience which OD must recognize and respect if it is to be successful. Some consequences of this experience and their implications for OD theory and technology will be discussed shortly, but first I want to comment on the definition of OD offered by these papers.

Sometimes the authors speak of OD as if it were a wholly agreed upon set of assumptions and procedures. But this idea is quickly dispelled by a reading of all the papers. Although there are unifying themes, the authors are as varied in their opinions about OD as were the legendary blind men describing the elephant. Moreover, it seems to me that, as with the blind men, differences between these authors arise primarily because they are describing different parts of the same animal.

Almost all the authors recognize a common dilemma of life in organizations, one that most readers probably have experienced. Surely you have been in groups where each of the people is competent, but as a group the members are simply unable to function effectively. Or perhaps you have witnessed instances in which perfectly reasonable solutions to organizational problems fail, or are never attempted, because of human failings, not technical ones. Both these events illustrate how a group's ability to function effectively is *not* equal to the sum of its members' technical skills. Other factors determine a group's ability to utilize available technical competence.

These events are familiar and past responses to them have varied. Some people have been inclined to act as if these kinds of problems are mended by changing formal organization structure and job design. Presumably, individual behavior passively responds to these objective alterations of organization life. Let us call this the "structural change approach." Other students of organization behavior, placing greater emphasis on the need for interpersonal skills, reject this approach and alternatively suggest that individual training in leadership, communication, conflict resolution, and other aspects of human relations is the road to organization success. Workshops designed to create these skills are regularly offered. Sadly, people who attend these workshops often return to their still unchanged organizations only to have their newly acquired inspiration, enthusiasm, and skills crushed by the weight of existing tradition. Let us call this the "individual change approach" and quickly add that neither this approach nor the structural change one characterizes OD as it is conceived by the papers in the present collection.

Changes in structure alone are explicitly rejected by Gabarro, Blumberg et al., and Schmuck. In addition, Schmuck, in his extremely interesting and informative paper, captures the sentiment of several authors when he says, "the dynamics of the group, *not the skills of individuals* in it, are seen as a major source of problems and as a primary determiner of the quality of solutions" (italics added). Yet techniques included in both the structural and individual change approaches are incorporated by the authors into what is called OD. But they are incorporated in a manner that totally alters their role in creating organization change.

Intact organization groups studying themselves at work on real organizational problems is the core of OD. *They work on themselves as they work on work.* As Schmuck says, "the group itself can learn to examine and improve its own resources and patterns of interaction." Interpersonal skills workshops and changes in structure may occur, but ordinarily that happens as a result of discoveries and decisions made by organization groups and their managers. Consequently, these changes and others concerned with improving organization effectiveness and individual satisfaction are instituted by the groups who will be affected by their introduction into the organization. In this context, without abdicating their operational responsibility, managers (e.g., leaders of community action groups, department heads, school principals, and school superintendents) place new emphasis on the role of facilitating the process of self-diagnosis and action-planning. In order to satisfactorily fulfill this role, OD consultants and managers use a variety of techniques, most of which are included in Blake and Mouton's D/D Matrix.

One positive feature of the D/D Matrix is that it calls attention to alternative processes of change involved in OD intervention tactics, i.e., the types of intervention column. But a matrix must do more than awaken attention to alternative possibilities. It must be accompanied by clear statements demarcating categories from one another. Some categories of the D/D Matrix overlap in potentially confusing ways: confrontations in intergroup situations (Class M interventions) can also be cathartic, which places them in Class C. Similarly, a catalytic intervention may have cathartic or confrontation qualities when, for example, "a number of people [engage] in deliberations about the character of their teamwork, intergroup contacts, or organizationwide activities." In these instances, the intervention may simultaneously belong in Classes B, G, and L. Similar problems of category overlap exist in a matrix proposed by Schmuck and Miles (1971), which I nevertheless recommend to readers because of its exceptionally comprehensive quality.

If used cautiously, these matrices can provide benefits inasmuch as they do catalog available intervention tactics in a practically useful fashion. But neither of them prescribes when tactics should or should not be used. Nor are there any formulas for determining when and how OD intervention tactics can be used in a way that is compatible with the idiosyncrasies of urban school systems.

## URBAN SCHOOL SYSTEMS: SPECIAL CLIENT CHARACTERISTICS

Three idiosyncratic qualities of urban school systems are briefly explored in this section. I call the subsections in which they are discussed (1) School Systems and Social Pathology; (2) The Principle of Flexible and Responsive Autonomy; and (3) Power—the Ambiguity of Organizational Authority. These topic headings do not subsume all the idiosyncrasies of urban school systems; nor are they necessarily the most important ones. But aspects of each appeared in several of the preceding papers and for that reason they were selected for attention here. To the extent that it is possible in the short space available to me, I will discuss the implications of these idiosyncrasies for OD theory and practice.

### SCHOOL SYSTEMS AND SOCIAL PATHOLOGY

For many years school systems were viewed by the public as one of the institutions that could provide their children with the necessary credentials for economic and social mobility. Because they possessed such pivotal power, whether real or imagined, they became the battleground for many of society's unresolved social conflicts. Politicians needing a cause are not likely to pass up an inflammable issue and, as Derr and Demb suggest, school systems are a handy-dandy vehicle for political gestures and power plays. Add to this the fact that in a society plagued by conflicts about racial, sexual, and economic discrimination, every operation involved in educating children becomes invested with special social significance, sometimes undeservedly. Decisions about grouping, time schedules, lunch programs, personnel assignments, district boundaries, guidance programs, testing, and record-keeping, which might otherwise be decided on the basis of assumed educational merit or administrative expediency, must now include a consideration of who will find the decision a sufficient reason for a *cause célèbre*. The benefits to society from this new consciousness may eventually be profound, but the stress it presently creates, added to the harassing activities of politicians and other interest groups, creates for urban school systems a continuous series of fires that need to be put out.

If an organization has been involved in an OD effort, and has attained the climate Schmuck describes and Blumberg et al. seem to have created at the Martin Luther King Elementary School, then the sudden need for fire-fighting will be responded to with the usual process of collaborative diagnosis and action, accompanied by a conscious concern for the group's management of its human resources. In today's world, however, urban school systems are rarely out of the fire-fighting business long enough to devote energy to starting a long-term OD effort. Can tactics be developed which respond to these fire-fighting needs and, simultaneously, create the basis for a more durable OD program? Fire-fighting tactics exist. For example, Derr and Demb briefly mention OT, "short-term intervention training, designed to help solve immediate organizational problems," and Beckhard (1967) has invented the "confrontation meeting" for this same purpose. But these events are most often isolated, one-shot affairs. Separated in time and place, they do not combine to create an OD culture. Consideration must be given to the possibility of strategically linking a number of fire-fighting tactics in order to provide the basis for long-term OD efforts in crisis-ridden urban school systems.

Instead of despairing about crisis management, it seems to me that OD practitioners could be more able to help if they recognized the client's position, *as it is being experienced,* and developed strategies which used the crisis atmosphere as a resource. Urban school systems may not be blameless for the costs their style of crisis management causes, but too often OD enthusiasts fail to see the objective need for fire-fighting and reject it as a possibility. Instead, they are intent on solving the organization's fundamental problems through a slow-moving, long-term OD effort, going from entry through contract, diagnosis, action-planning and fol-low-up. Organization resistance to this approach, because of the need for relief of immediate pain, is often wrongly interpreted as deep-seated resistance to change of any kind because an OD enthusiast suffers under the "helper's fallacy": "Your inability to receive that which I am about to give is your fault."

### THE PRINCIPLE OF FLEXIBLE AND RESPONSIVE AUTONOMY

One extremely important idea contained in Gabarro's article is that the need for subunit autonomy is *not* equal on every occasion. Building on Lawrence and Lorsch's model of organizations, he argues that task requirements and environmental conditions combine to alter the optimally desirable level of subunit autonomy in different parts of an organization. At times, OD practitioners overlook this idea. With myopic focus on the principles and research that underlie participative management, they argue that commitment to decisions, individual satisfaction, and effective problem-solving all require regular, active participation of a broad range of people in organization decisions.

Derr and Demb observe a contrary condition in schools, noting that there is a general lack of required interdependence. Thus,

Those aspects of OD technology which were designed to deal with situations where the level of required interdependence (collaboration) is high are rightfully regarded with skepticism by many school people. The major objective of schools, the teaching and transmittal of knowledge, occurs in the highly autonomous classroom situations.

I believe that one reason for this skepticism is the OD practitioner's not-too-well-hidden assumption that "autonomy is always bad; active, collaborative interdependence is always good." As Gabarro tells us, theory, research, and practical experience indicate that this assumption is wrong.

Once again, instead of despairing about high subunit autonomy, OD enthusiasts might begin to develop tactics which suit the culture and simultaneously lessen the dangers of this organization arrangement. One such tactic is Roger Harrison's (1972) "Role Negotiation," which incidentally was developed while he was consulting with school officials.

Two dangers of high subunit autonomy seem obvious and should be of concern to OD practitioners and educators alike: (1) Autonomous organization arrangements, like most others, have a way of becoming inflexible despite changing demands. OD interventions are needed which will enhance the benefits of autonomous structure and, at the same time, create the psychological and operational basis for changing the structure should that become necessary. (2) Autonomous organization arrangements often create waste because information flow is restricted. OD interventions must be developed which operate within the context of an autonomous structure and yet make certain that the right information gets to the right place at the right time.

## POWER: THE AMBIGUITY OF ORGANIZATIONAL AUTHORITY

Managers of most commercial firms are in a position to decide whether an OD project should be started and, once started, whether it should proceed. If they have a board of directors, they ordinarily do not seek its permission for the project. Moreover, the decision to begin an OD project does not interest inanimate objects like fork lift trucks, oil, and missiles. Customers scarcely show any greater degree of concern. Whatever its costs may be, the centralization of authority in commercial firms works to the advantage of OD programs, initially when the program is beginning, and subsequently when changes are introduced. Only occasionally in urban school systems is the decision-making authority so unambiguously invested in a few people.

As Derr and Demb say, urban school systems are vulnerable to pressure from a number of sources because of their product and their task. Their decisions are reviewed and influenced by a number of parties, including students, community groups, unions and other teacher groups, administrators, members of the board (who almost always have a political constituency to satisfy), news reporters, and various self-accredited educators.

OD is not only time consuming and expensive (two issues which will surely arouse someone's ire); if successful, it frequently involves a clarification and realignment of power and authority. For a variety of reasons, this possibility is often experienced as a threat, and resistance is considerable. For some individuals and groups, the experience of threat may be realistic because they exercise a degree of control and influence which is excessive and inappropriate and needs to be diminished if the organization is to function effectively. These are the times when OD practitioners suffer their worst defeats. Because of their intellectual and moral commitments they are wedded to intervention techniques which are ill equipped to successfully confront self-seeking people who have vested interests in maintaining the status quo.

In working with urban school systems, OD practitioners must become proactive and use techniques involving both direct advocacy and the manipulation of power. Two examples of these techniques, used by clients, *not* consultants, are evident in Blumberg et al. In one case, teachers, feeling that their recent gains were in jeopardy, organized a political pressure group. In the second case, a black principal stimulated community interest by engaging in a perfidious political ploy. These techniques can have undesirable by-products, and thought should be given to developing procedures which motivate intransigent people to yield to change, while minimizing dysfunctional anger.

OD's success in other organization contexts can become the basis of its failure in urban school systems, if there is a rigid adherence to previously useful techniques. Idiosyncrasies of this new organization demand adaptive innovation of OD principles. The papers by Blumberg et al., and Schmuck, particularly, represent departures from traditional OD procedures. Now, guided by principles and values of OD, attention must be given to the creation of techniques for organization fire-fighting, working with highly autonomous subunits, and dealing with power in organizations.

## REFERENCES

BECKHARD, R. (1967) "The confrontation meeting." Harvard Business Rev. 45, 2: 149-155.

HARRISON, R. (1972) "Role negotiation: a tough minded approach to team development," in W. W. Burke and H. A. Hornstein (eds.) The Social Technology of Organization Development. Fairfax, Va.: NTL Learning Resources Corporation.

SCHMUCK, R. A. and M. B. MILES (1971) Organization Development in Schools. Palo Alto, Calif.: National Press Books.

# DEVELOPING LEADERSHIP TRAINING FOR BIG-CITY PRINCIPALS

MARK R. SHEDD
CHARLES C.D. HAMILTON
MARK MUNGER
*Graduate School of Education*
*Harvard University*

**The urban school administrator** finds an increasing number of tools to approach the complex situations with which he or she deals. One such tool which may be increasingly helpful for the urban administrator is the theory and practice of organizational development. Knowledge of OD theory helps one to consider the consequences of organizational choices, and acting on methodology may bring the disparate parts of a school system into a more coherent and cohesive unit.

In Philadelphia we used one kind of organizational training with our principals and district-level administrators. It was one approach among many to improve middle management capabilities, but there may be some learnings in it which might be appropriate or adaptable for other situations.

The new superintendent in 1967, with a new school board, encountered many of the characteristic problems of large,

AUTHORS' NOTE: *This discussion grew out of a series of conversations between Mark R. Shedd, former Superintendent of Schools in Philadelphia; Charles C.D. Hamilton, an organizational development consultant who was associated with the IAAD in Philadelphia; and Mark T. Munger, an educator with an interest in organizational development.*

urban school systems. Students were alienated and performing poorly, minority groups faced discriminatory situations and attitudes, curricular irrelevance had become an issue, teachers and communities were disaffected, and an inbred administrative structure had become overcentralized.

Our staff began to work in a variety of areas; we sought multiple approaches to deal with some of the interrelated symptoms of our basic problems. Among our most important targets were administrative reorganization and an improvement of management at every level of the system. It was within the context of managerial retraining that we thought we perceived a utility for some of the theories and methodologies associated with organizational development.

Accordingly, we made a structural intervention in the school and established an Institute for Advanced Administrative Development. It was through the Institute that we began to work on some of the interpersonal aspects of managerial behavior, particularly as regards up-down communication. Before examining the IAAD, its purposes and its work, it is important to establish its context, to place the Institute within the spectrum of change efforts in the school system.

We had to make efforts to relieve overcrowding and to think about retiring some of the older buildings, and established an office of capital planning and development, with extensive liaison with the city planning commission. We created a department of physical plant and program planning with a research and evaluation capacity. We introduced PPBS and Project Management concepts to key personnel, to bolster financial and administrative capabilities. Sophisticated data-processing techniques were instituted in payroll, financial management, personnel, and pupil accounting. We tried to institutionalize student and community participation in conjunction with attempts at administrative decentralization, and began to push for improved links between the Central Office and the field.

Simultaneously the School District attempted to incorporate black and urban studies programs, and scrutinized its personnel policies with special attention to minority recruitment. We supported what we hoped would be innovative alternative programs such as the Pennsylvania Advancement School and the Parkway Program, and the system made large numbers of direct grants to schools and individual teachers. A Student Bill of Rights and Responsibilities was adopted and implemented.

We tried to increase public knowledge of and public access to the system. Through "open mike" radio shows, open and televised board hearings, and other forums, we hoped to make the system more visible and more open.

In particular, we saw a need to reach principals and administrators on a district level, and to assist them in using their own resources to accomplish their own goals. Too many competent and capable people were waiting for direction from the central office instead of using their own initiative. As often happens, bureaucratic channels had become clogged, and information going up and down the system had become self-protective and inaccurate. Individual and collective performances suffered.

We wanted to use OD to open up the system, to influence as many levels of the system as possible. We used it as one tactic among many, but because of its inherent nature, a tactic which would enable us to surface important problems and collaboratively arrive at what we hoped would be creative solutions.

In introducing an OD approach we felt we had to be explicit about our reasons for doing so, and to be very clear about our values. Behind our desire for change lay the following beliefs.

We believed that effective people were not working well together. The school system was not serving its different populations, it was out of phase. In order to educate children and revitalize communities, the system required change. We thought it could move and we tried to establish some different norms.

- Human differences are to be recognized, acknowledged, and accepted.
- It is all right to be different.
- We can agree to disagree.
- It is possible to set aside hostilities and explore areas of mutual self-interest.
- If we increase our own interpersonal competence and become aware of our own resourcefulness, we will be able to share commonalities and build coalitions to achieve our common goals.

It was upon such values and assumptions that we sought funding for a program in management training which would focus on utilization of resources, negotiation skills, conflict management, and school-community relations. Open to question at the time, in a school system beset by racial and ethnic antagonisms, were the credibility and effectiveness of administrators, and the usefulness of a participatory approach to problem-solving for people who had previously been shut out of decision-making. Underlying the choice of an organizational, human relations approach and of primary importance to Philadelphia, was the symbolism of getting a process started, of beginning a dialogue between principals and members of the local school family, which would enable them to act together.

## OBJECTIVES

Our goals fit within the galaxy of common OD goals, yet we were aware that for our purposes, an OD program was not an end. Because of the political context into which we had come, we hoped to make our management training as pragmatic and useful as possible. We were very much aware of the environment, and how it influenced our principals and district administrators. In our training we wanted to emphasize the situational aspects of their work as a base upon which they could build. We felt a need to help them understand the uniqueness and idiosyncrasies of their own school communities.

Our intent was to help them learn by exposing them to a technology taken from organizational development experience. What technology was it? First, it was to increase their awareness of themselves, how other people perceived them. Second, it was to enhance their own abilities to experience other people and be open to learning from them. Third, we hoped to improve their capacity to communicate, to be open and confrontive with those around them. We hoped that they would learn in these areas, as others have before them, through experience, through intensive sessions with varieties of people learning about each other through sharing their problems.

We anticipated that a laboratory methodology would help people in looking at their own behavior, that anything that happened would be considered part of the learning experience, and that competent consultants could establish an atmosphere in which our administrators could take a hard look at real differences. We hoped to support and encourage conflict and confrontation, believing that there are times when conflict is likely to occur when mutual self-interest does not overlap, and that conflict can be healthy.

More traditional OD interventions start at the very top of an organizational structure, and attempt to influence the behavior of top management. The assumption is that change at the top will influence and initiate change throughout the entire organization. Recognizing that, we tried to pay attention to our own behavior at the Cabinet level. But we believed that money and resources would have more impact spent at school and district level. Our goal was increased autonomy for districts, and we felt that district leadership teams would profit from the training we hoped to give them.

Another fundamental principle of OD theory and practice, data collection, was modified. We did not have an exhaustive data collection process, upon which consultants would collaborate in diagnoses of our problems. Each district generated its own data, but there was not a systematic, systemwide data collection process.

The Institute we established was a training vehicle for a number of small organizations—the districts. While we viewed it as a total system intervention, its work was downward, a penetration into the system, rather than horizontal. Organizational purists might hold that our efforts were not of sufficient scope nor intensity to produce valuable results or valuable learning for other systems. Our view is that nothing will change for children and teachers unless some training and support is given principals. One of our operating principles— that management training which raises levels of competence must be practical, of day-to-day substance, and based on our criteria of what districts should consider—is less collaborative than one might like. Similarly, our methodology was based on simulations concerning what was happening "back home," in the schools. Our human relations effort was geared to team-building—taking units of people who had histories together and working with them to become collectively more competent, attempting to increase each individual's sense of self-worth. These are departures from total-system interventions, but we feel that there is something of value in our effort.

## THE INSTITUTE

Our effort centers in the Institute and in its alternative model to training. We were searching for ways to practice autonomy as well as preach it, to have our training agency operate independently with districts we hoped would become more independent of central office domination and control. To support this idea, we established the IAAD as a separate entity within the system, a separate entity with direct access to the superintendent. We committed money, time, and resources to the Institute to indicate our belief in the value of its task. In considering the role of the Institute before it came into being, we thought of two points in particular. First, we wanted authority for the expenditure of moneys at a district level to reside with the Institute and the districts. District people had to know that they had a say in how the money allocated toward their training was going to be spent. A second kind of empowerment had to do with personnel, both of the Institute and the consultants it would later hire. We involved the Principal's Association in the selection of the codirectors (the leadership), so that the administration of the Institute would be known and familiar, and we accepted the choices of the principals. We also wanted the Institute directors to have considerable latitude with money. In the matter of consulting fees, we wanted to be able to attract competent consultants. Our aim was to get good people, and if that meant being competitive with the private sector, so be it.

We began to think about the Institute in specific terms, in particular with reference to its cost and funding, with the following estimates and assumptions in mind. We had a critical need for well-trained, well-prepared administrative leaders. Within each school district we wanted to generate district commitment to learning goals, community goals, and administrative goals. We wanted a program which would have broad and rapid effect, we hoped to train at least one-third of almost 300 principals in the first year. We hoped to relieve some of the financial burden of the program by employing central office expertise, resources, and personnel in lieu of outside help wherever it might be feasible. We thought there would be some interesting and important learnings for Central Office staff who would work in the field, and be at least indirectly involved in the leadership training through their contact with field operations. We drew upon resources from other ongoing Philadelphia projects, as we anticipated that administrators from all levels would be trained within one training cycle. In addition, we planned for structured follow-ups to the training within each district, that a trained cadre of people would form a "critical mass" for change.

We conceived this program to train principals to a new role concept, a role explored and defined by the principals themselves. We believed that as managers they were capable of using resources to accomplish their own goals, but in order to do that they might wish to think about changes in their managerial styles. We hoped to reduce reliance upon directives from the central office and to decrease their tendency to issue directives to people in their own schools. We hoped that they might develop a more independent management mode. As line officers, we had to involve them in our own notion of management objectives for the total system. We believed that additional knowledge in four crucial areas must be made available to them, for them to sample and adapt, as they found the content useful. These four areas were budget-planning, institutional decision-making, community participation, and interpersonal skills. Finally, we assumed that training would be more valuable were it linked to team-building, if administrative units who would return to districts working together could develop some cooperative planning and implementation strategies within and among the schools of each district.

The task of the IAAD was to design and operate training programs for the intentions and objectives outlined above. The Institute was to provide expertise for field personnel in the areas of budget planning, organizational development, negotiations, group dynamics, instructional alternatives, child growth and development, and management skills. The Institute was to identify resources for the improvement of managerial skills.

In addition the Institute was to provide assistance in th
evaluation of the effectiveness of planning and trainin
programs, and provide support, technical and financial, fo
districts in the design, operation, and evaluation of individua
school planning and training programs.

With funding from the Ford Foundation and funding an
support from the School District of Philadelphia, the IAAI
began its first training programs in 1969. It was an exercise i
decentralization and management accountability, as its wor
lay in districts to which it could provide assistance but no
overt administrative direction. One of the critical factor
affecting the establishment and workings of the Institute wa
that it was not dealing with purely educational issues, bu
rather with administrators as individuals, encouraging the
to become open, risk-taking, and confident. They had t
value that experience and behavior; it could not be impose
on them. The role of principal in the system had change
particularly in relation to the union leadership. We hope
that the principals would respond to the opportunity t
consider new management roles, to develop new skills an
technologies, and to deal with some crucial issues, in whic
they might learn from constituents and get support fror
each other. It is important to stress the voluntary, autonc
mous nature of this process. We could not legislate it.

The proposal for the IAAD had come from the Superir
tendent's Office. Data for training, and leadership for th
Institute had come from the Principal's Association. /
planning committee had functioned in a reasonably repr
sentative, democratic way to develop a rationale for autor
omy for each district. It was a consciously decentralize
effort to protect a decentralized idea—choices were in th
hands of districts. Principals on a district level could operat
within organizational boundaries by applying for trainin
funds from the Institute to design their own trainin
experiences. These experiences turned out to be quit
different for different districts, just as districts evolve

dissimilar planning mechanisms. This was desirable. In fact, after a series of workshops run for districts in the first year of the Institute, in the second year the eight district superintendents took responsibility themselves.

In one district, eleven principals and the district superintendent developed a year-long training model, with a one-month intensive training phase. This pattern generally held true, with participants going off site for a residential period, and then continuing to talk and plan outside of the normal school context. The Institute would help administer the training, provide materials and consultants, assist the district with its follow-up and evaluation. There was no single design for training. However, each training cycle shared a number of common characteristics. Each focused on potential changes in district educational programs, in the process of program development, and changing roles within the system. In the training-group process techniques seemed to strengthen team relationships, and made new demands on administrators on both district and central office levels for more effective leadership.

## "OUR OWN RESOURCES"

One significant aspect of the training for us was how it got done. In an urban system so large, so complex, with many people working fifty-hour weeks and a "business as usual" attitude somewhat pervasive, it required energy to initiate the IAAD. Management training demanded a new training procedure, and here the role of Central Office personnel became essential. We wanted to demonstrate that we could pull off this type of training within our system, and do it with quality, while still continuing to operate. We had to pull some people away for a solid month, with all the implications of their absence from critical posts. We tried to mobilize the resources of the total system to deal with the exigencies of district training, and so serve as a model for districts doing training of their own. Accordingly, we brought Central Office staff out into the field, to assume some of the responsibilities of those involved in the training. We called on available resources to perform creatively in carrying out new and sometimes different responsibilities. The concept was that we already were carrying a spare tire, we did not have to go out and buy one.

This placement of downtown people in the field had a number of ramifications. First, the principals were somewhat apprehensive. How could somebody else do their jobs? Did that mean that they themselves were not necessary? What would the other person find out about them in their absence? How could the school function without them? All those questions had to be confronted.

Second, the Central Office staff were asking the same kinds of questions as regarded their own jobs. How can it get done without me? Am I so dispensable? What will people learn when I am not there to protect my territory? Will I be any good in the field, as there are problems here I am not sure I understand?

We were trying to indicate that many people had latent capabilities, and that once a break was made with the ordinary way of doing things, that people would react imaginatively and capably. We believe that the Central Office staff became much more familiar with the field activities which they experienced firsthand. They would later become more responsive in facilitating the real focus of the system, the schools. We think that the principals were able to conceive of their roles in a different way. If the school could continue to operate without them, were they not freed up to take a more creative and more flexible role in the life of the school? People in the field and in the Central Office began to look at one another differently, as they considered their colleagues as resources and supports.

For the broader school community, their participation in the process, in the workshops, gave them insights into the workings of schools they had not had previously. The inclusion of students and parents and community people in some of the training sessions worked both ways. It increased the awareness of the administrators, and at the same time made the community more aware of some of the constraints of the system. In addition, the invitation of union representatives helped what in some cases had been uneasy combatants to better explore and understand each others' personalities and positions.

The perception that people could begin to be sources of help to each other was one of the biggest benefits of the training, as reported by many of the participants. It is important to consider here the important role of the consultants in the work of the Institute. The Institute hired competent consultants, with particular attention to their values and to the level of their commitment to the work. The districts, some of which later interviewed their own consultants, and the Institute itself were conscious of the kind of person they wanted. The consultants who worked with the districts brought what might be described as an NTL community development approach, an activist orientation which influenced their approach to their work and the individuals and the districts.

The consultants were more involved in the training aspect of the Institute than in the design. As each district evolved its own training package, the consultant worked with group techniques and group activities, centered around a pragmatic approach to solving some of the problems of the district. The consultants were confrontive; one of their tasks was to help administrators and community see the value of each others' participation in important decisions. As third parties, the consultants were able to employ a variety of strategies, from collaboration to power bargaining, to help people better understand and use each other as resources. The consultants adjusted their own training capabilities to encourage productive conflict and confrontation. The notion of a third party was particularly helpful as participants learned negotiation skills.

Looking from the role of the consultants to the total work of the Institute, it is possible to see some omissions and some weaknesses. There were a number of missing ingredients. There was not an integrated design for the entire Institute; autonomy was so valued that the districts often engaged in very different activites. There was not systemwide clarity of objectives, again made difficult by the disparity of experiences and intentions at a district level. Part of the value training was what the consultants brought to it, and district size mitigated against all administrators and subgroups being able to become involved in the training. More than 41% of the administrators had some form of participation in year one. The research component of the Institute was not able to make as much use of the data it collected as we would have liked.

We do feel, however, that there were a number of significant learnings for us, both in the content of the Institute and the process by which it happened. It is important to share some of these learnings, as some of them may be generalizable to other systems. It is difficult to distinguish what was learned from how it was learned, but that was one of the aims of the Institute, to help people become more independent by treating them with the respect accorded to independent people.

Although it is difficult to measure, we think that the participants in the training, in most of the districts, found latent capabilities in themselves and in their colleagues. Statements such as "my feelings of self-esteem increased, and my feelings of respect from the system increased as I was able to improve my skills," or "I know my colleagues now as people, as sources of support, as sounding boards," were somewhat representative of what we heard. Just as individuals found resources in themselves, schools found new abilities in the school "family," and the school became a microcosm of the system. Just as the schools found more abilities to handle more problems without going downtown for a decision, so the system found that it had resources within itself it had not tapped before.

We began to rethink some of our other training models, and saw some flexibility in our relationships with outside consultants. It is the notion that we could do it within the existing constraints of the system which we found exciting. We could achieve specific training goals within the constraints we know, and in so doing, alter the constraints.

We developed, at a central office and a district level, a faith in others' abilities to make responsible choices. Here the methodology was important. We experienced a kind of adult education, with which professional people could document new learnings for themselves, and think about the application of those learnings. Our principals responded well to responsibility.

We think we perceived other changes, particularly a chance for people to begin dialogues between schools and communities. Because of the involvement of local people in the training with the district principals, both parties were able to acquire a common vocabulary which would enable them to build upon the dialogue. There were, as always, some unintended consequences. Some districts learned through the training that things often heat up before they cool down, but we are satisfied that the conflicts that surfaced became more manageable.

Within the groups of administrators there were some significant developments in team-building. Groups of principals came to know each other singly and collectively, and found they shared a number of common problems. Going after their commonalities they developed an internal change momentum. Greater district autonomy means change for the central office, and the increased familiarity with district problems on the part of some central office staff helped to lubricate some of the changes. In living with autonomy, the Central Office also faces improved negotiation skills on the part of the districts. A new ability to negotiate makes collaboration somewhat easier, but also can lead to power-bargaining strategies where roles have changed.

We believe that the sense of autonomy, coupled with team-building skills, is the basis for any meaningful effort at decentralization. As an example of that, each group which finished a training cycle met with the Superintendent to discuss the experience and the problems which had surfaced. We began to get more accurate information, upon which we could base long-range planning, as a result of the new openness and risk-taking.

Just as it was important to follow up the process by dealing with critical issues and continuing leadership training, it was important to use a sense of "creative hindsight" in looking at the Institute. We needed to be consistent and to model the behavior we were advocating. We needed to think out the choice points, and plan for decisions we knew would have to be made. Just as we needed to think through the training cycles, we needed to be flexible ourselves, and adjust to situations we had not anticipated in the way we hoped administrators in the field would adjust to similar situations.

## CONCLUSION

It is tempting to oversimplify the dynamics of the process we began with the Institute. We think we had a broad systemwide impact by creating it, and by supporting districts as they used it to meet some of their own ends. It is only one effort in a series of efforts to increase the capabilities of administrators and to improve the responsiveness of the system. Just as the training represented one kind of organizational development approach to a school system, so does the organizational development approach represent one of a mix of technical skills needed to work within a complex system. We would assert that the more valuable the training is to become, the more it is rooted in a practical approach to solving important problems. The technologies we used to help people focus on their own behavior are important for improved management. We think that organizational development strategies can become one of the important tools for the urban administrator, and we look forward to its increased utilization.

# ORGANIZATIONAL TRAINING FOR IMPROVING RACE RELATIONS

JOE E. GENTRY
*Experimental Schools Project*
*School District of Greenville County, South Carolina*

J. FOSTER WATKINS
*School of Education*
*Auburn University*

**The process of desegrating** public schools in the Southern United States reached a climax with the opening of schools for the 1970-1971 academic year. Through the initial response to the "with all deliberate speed" mandate, the desegration process gained some momentum. The Supreme Court again exerted a powerful influence in the matter by ruling that a "freedom of choice" plan was not acceptable since it had not dismantled the dual school system. Immediately the lower courts and the U.S. Department of Health, Education and Welfare (HEW) began to apply pressure to school districts to produce terminal desegregation plans which were to be implemented in the 1970-1971 school year.

In many cases, these plans called for reorganization of individual schools. Such reorganized or reconstituted schools reflected different grade assignment patterns, different instructional patterns, different student bodies, different administrative arrangements, and substantially revised faculty assignments.[1] These changes were made with varying degrees

AUTHORS' NOTE: *The research on which this article is based was the doctoral study of Mr. Gentry. The study was directed by Mr. Watkins at Auburn University. The organizational training experiences were supported by the funds under Title IV of the Civil Rights Act of 1964*

f involvement on the part of those affected. In some cases
principals and teachers had no contact until the beginning of
preschool planning activities prior to the opening of school in
August 1970. In a few situations desegregation plans were
changed by the Court a matter of days before the scheduled
opening of school. This resulted in unanticipated transfer of
staff and students and in some cases even caused a delay in
the opening of school.

Authority relations, communication networks, formal
groupings, and even informal groupings faced change and
stress. The development of effective working relationships
was no small task for a biracial faculty, who for the most part
had never worked together for the primary task of educating
black and white students in the same schools. How is such a
team effort developed? What are the components which are
essential if such a group is to function? Can the time required
to develop effective organizational processes be speeded up?

In seeking answers to these questions and a vehicle through
which to accomplish needed change in the norms and
procedures of a school, interest was aroused in work which
had been done in the field of organizational training at the
Center for Advanced Study of Educational Administration
(CASEA) at the University of Oregon (Schmuck and Runkel,
1970). Here researchers had been attempting to improve
organizational characteristics of a school by improving the
interpersonal communication skills and the organizational
problem-solving ability of the school staff. Techniques were
employed which focused on the improvement of communication in groups through a modified laboratory method
involving a total task-oriented unit.

The CASEA intervention stressed the importance of
effective organizational problem-solving. The training efforts

through the Auburn Center for Assisting School Systems with Problems
Occasioned by Desegregation. At the time of the study, Mr. Gentry was
a doctoral research assistant with the Center and Mr. Watkins was the
Associate Director of the Center.

in problem-solving, however, seemed minimal. A method of problem-solving through group discussion developed at Auburn University seemed to fill a need in this area of training. It involves "informal but orderly conversation to decide how to achieve a common goal by overcoming the barriers to it, or to establish new goals in the light of these barriers" (Smith, 1965: 30). The pattern of constructive thinking is employed with discussion problems, and the strengths of the entire group are maximized in seeking solutions to problems.

Here seemed to be a combination of methods worthy of utilizing in attempting to produce a school organization capable of coping with the numerous stresses applied by desegregation. The Auburn Center for Assisting School Systems with Problems Occasioned by Desegregation (the Auburn Center), a Title IV center authorized under the Civil Rights Act of 1964, arranged to test an intervention based on the CASEA design with expanded emphasis on problem-solving skills in order to determine if this type of organizational training seemed to enhance the development of organizational processes in a reconstituted school as these processes were uniquely impacted upon by the movement toward unitary schools.

It was decided to field-test such an intervention in a medium-sized, rather industrialized city in Alabama which had begun to feel the influence of the influx of blacks from the rural areas of the county. The school system was approached with the idea of conducting organizational training in a school in which the impact of desegregation was expected to be great. After the consideration of several schools by the administrators of the school system, it was decided in July 1970 that the project would be located in a primary (grades one through three) school. As was the case in most school systems throughout the Southern United States, the project school had been scheduled for significant changes.

Prior to the 1970-1971 school year the project school had served an all-black student body in grades one through seven.

For two years a few white faculty members referred to as "cross-over" teachers had worked in this school of 600 students and eighteen faculty members. The superintendent and his administrative staff, since coming to the school system in 1968, had achieved rapid change in the instructional program. Several additional innovative instructional practices were planned for the 1970-1971 school year in anticipation of the need to intensify the system's movement toward an individualized instructional program because of desegregation.

A student body of 700 in grades one through three and a faculty of 24 were scheduled to be housed in the school. The racial composition of the student body was to be approximately 60% white and 40% black. The racial composition of the faculty was to be 75% white and 25% black. The staff members were unacquainted with each other for the most part. Several of the faculty, having been employed through the central office, were unknown to the principal. The former principal, a black, was to remain in his position in one of the few situations where a black principal was retained in a majority white school. Although he had served as a school administrator for several years, the principal had little formal training in school administration. A wide age differential existed among the faculty, as the reassignment of teachers within the system resulted in a group of experienced teachers selecting to work together in this school. Another substantial group of teachers was either new to the system or had been in the system four years or less.

The challenge confronting this reconstituted school was evident. Curricular and instructional changes leading toward an individualized instructional program posed a substantial problem to the school staff. Adjustments to new administrative procedures, to new coworkers, to a new setting, and to a greater degree of biracial working relationships compounded the problems. It was apparent that this school faced a monumental task.

## STATEMENT OF THE PROBLEM

The purposes of the study were to record the experience of an organizational training workshop conducted for the staff of a reconstituted school, to assess the strengths and weaknesses of that training, and to document the impact of such training upon the organization and its individual members. Inherent in the purposes of the investigation was the assumption that participation in a concentrated two-week workshop experience, which focused upon interpersonal relations, communication skills, group discussion, and problem-solving abilities, would result in some organizational impact. The investigation sought particularly to determine whether organizational training facilitates the desegregation process and at the same time aids the problem-solving process dealing with curricular, instructional, and organizational change.

The general design of the study was two-pronged: (1) a case study which ferreted out what actually happened in the experimental school as a result of the workshop experiences and (2) a quasi-experimental-control design which looked at change in objective data collected in the experimental and control schools.

One school in the same school system served as an in-system control school for the experimental school. Four external control schools participated in the investigation through the objective instrumentation. These schools were also primary schools in eastern Alabama and generally had characteristics similar to those of the control school.

It was anticipated that the training would affect the organizational climate of the school, the degree of participation by the staff in the organizational processes, the attitudes of the staff concerning leadership, the interpersonal relations of the staff, and the quality of meetings and communication within the school. To measure the effect of the training, emphasis was placed primarily through the case study on what actually happened within the school. Efforts were made to assess both short-range and more enduring outcomes through the use of developed questionnaires, structured interviews, and systematic observations of the ongoing program. In addition, several measuring instruments were employed in order to obtain an objective assessment of the impact of training upon the staff of the experimental school and to compare this with schools not undergoing the training. Instruments utilized in this aspect of the study included Halpin and Croft's Organizational Climate Description Questionnaire (OCDQ), sociometric choice scales, the Rokeach Dogmatism Scale—Form E, the Haiman Leadership Attitude (LA) Scale, and the Staff Meetings in This School (SMTS) instrument as modified by CASEA.

## THE WORKSHOP EXPERIENCE

In preparing the design for the training in the summer workshop the Auburn trainers drew heavily upon the experiences of CASEA in organizational training (Schmuck and Runkel, 1970). Three major deviations from the CASEA training approach were made. First, the workshop was designed for a ten-day period rather than six days. Second, after the third day the problem-solving strategy was developed around the theory and rationale of Smith (1965) rather than the CASEA problem-solving sequence. Finally, problem-solving received considerably more emphasis than in the CASEA training.

Increased emphasis on the problem-solving process was deemed necessary in order to develop that skill to the point that the entire faculty would be capable of functioning as a contributing member in any group problem-solving experience. It was accepted that this skill was necessary in facultywide issues concerning student, teacher, and relevant administrative areas as well as in team and group instructional planning sessions. As the problem-solving process was stressed, constant reinforcement of communication, effective meeting, openness, and feedback skills were reinforced.

The workshop design employed three primary thrusts. The first three days concentrated on communication skills. Activities designed to promote consensus-building, helping relationships, effective communication, paraphrasing, and feedback were employed. A vacation resort away from the work scene was chosen for the first three days of the workshop. Participants stayed overnight, thus promoting more informal communication and personal interaction among participants and trainers.

The next phase of the training was conducted on the campus of Auburn University which was within commuting distance for the participants. The first three days of the on-campus workshop dealt with the theory and practice of the skills of problem-solving through discussion. Identification of goals, resolving differences, group leadership, and value clarification exercises were conducted. Participants engaged in practice discussions while trainers monitored and critiqued the process.

The final four days of the training focused on the task of solving problems which the staff perceived they would actually face at their school during the coming year. Specific action strategies were developed. Again, trainers assisted the various task groups with the problem-solving process.

The three-member training team included one black considering the biracial composition of the trainees. The trainers took a positive approach to racial understanding during the workshop. Cooperative work on the problems at hand was conducted without regard to race. Care was taken, however, to rotate groups so that each person worked with every other participant and every trainer. References to racial understandings were made when deemed appropriate by the trainers or members of the school staff. No concerted effort was made to avoid such issues nor to pursue them unnecessarily. This was in keeping with a positive approach to increased racial understanding through planned biracial experiences and reflected the philosophical position of the Auburn Center's staff as they worked systematically toward improved race relations in their several programs.

One specific example which illustrates the treatment of racial concerns during the workshop experience was that one discussion group voluntarily elected to discuss "How can we achieve effective biracial communication in our school?" On another occasion individuals utilized newsprint, paints, magic markers, or crayons to create scenes depicting their expectations about the opening of school. Designated subgroups were then asked to connect these drawings to form a mural and to discuss them with the total group. Several sequences dealt with concerns about race relations in their newly desegregated situation. These were handled openly and thoroughly by the groups.

## CONCLUSIONS OF THE STUDY

The dual nature of the design employed in the study allowed for utilization of two types of data in drawing conclusions. The case study provided a subjective approach while the instrumentation injected a degree of objectivity. Conclusions which were supported by the findings of the study are discussed with primary consideration given to the facilitation of the desegregation process, in keeping with the focus of this article.

(1) The organizational training workshop had a meaningful, immediate, short-range impact on the principal and the staff of the experimental school.

All attempts to evalute the workshop experience indicated a positive impact of the training. Objective data obtained from participants rated the workshop well above the usual level of expectation held for educational workshops and demonstrated that the training goals were achieved to a high degree. Participants cited a feeling of excitement relative to the new school year because of the new ways they anticipated working together as a staff. During the workshop experience, the principal had demonstrated a willingness to accept the ideas of others even when they were in opposition to his own. This fact was commented upon favorably by other staff members.

Anxiety over working in a biracial situation had been reduced. In interviews conducted as part of the case study, both black and white staff members talked of the excellent relationships between the races. Some black teachers identified a higher degree of openness existing between coworkers this year as compared to previous years. A number of teachers of both races spoke of how anxieties over desegregation problems had decreased because of the workshop experiences. The principal was pleased at the quality of the interracial relationships existing among the staff. He was generous in his praise of the workshop as a primary reason for these relationships. He felt that the workshop provided the basis for a smooth transition into the biracial teaching situation.

Information gained by CASEA visitors to the system in late spring in their evaluative discussions with the superintendent provided additional support for the impact of the project in this area. He expressed his belief that the project had played "an important part in what he perceived to be a smooth transition in the desegregation process." He admitted readily that the anticipated problems of a race relations nature, which had prompted the selection of the particular school to participate in the project, had not materialized.

During his frequent visits to the school, the researcher was continually impressed with the high quality of interpersonal relationships among the staff. Only on his final visit to the school was he made aware of dissatisfactions with racial implications. The dissatisfactions stemmed from the principal's performance ratings of individual teachers. Some white teachers felt the principal was racially biased toward those of the black race on these ratings.

The objective data furnished by the OCDQ in the experimental school revealed significant differences in the perceptions of the races on two dimensions of the principal's behavior and no significant differences on the dimensions of peer group behavior. Initially the races viewed staff meetings in a similar way but, on a final expression, blacks viewed them more favorably. The tendency was greater on original choices to choose more preferred coworkers from the opposite race than on final choices. One indication that may be drawn from the objective data is that immediately following the workshop training, race made less difference in the way the staff functioned than it did near the close of the school year—a point which is possibly explained by related findings which are discussed below.

(2) The organizational training workshop had a differential effect on the principal and the staff over the course of the school year immediately following the training.

There were attempts during the first part of the school year to put the theory and ideas of the workshop into practice. Most of these attempts resulted from actions initiated by the teaching staff. Examples of these attempts included such actions as planning for improved utilization of instructional aides, implementing improved lunchroom and teachers' lounge conditions, requesting action on numerous areas of concern with building routines, participating in planning the follow-up organizational training session, and establishing procedures for better interpersonal relations within the faculty. A number of teachers identified carry-over of workshop ideas into the classroom. Members of the teaching staff played a leadership role in forming and keeping a principal's advisory group functioning. This group assumed unusual responsibilities during an extended illness of the principal. The teaching staff performed exceptionally well in the preparation of a school policy handbook.

Recognizing that the high expectations they held for new ways of working together as a staff were not being met, various teachers reported that the staff was determined not to let their plans die. They recognized that the establishment of effective ways to gain participation and involvement in the organization would take time. The staff further recognized the unusual pressures upon the principal resulting from the reconstituted nature of school.

The principal apparently was anxious initially to involve the staff in organizational problem-solving. The final session of the workshop had been designed to utilize the group and its group process skills in the preplanning activities for the opening of school. The principal later reported that the group process ideas had to be abandoned because of the pressures of the opening of school but that "he was going to follow through with plans as soon as things settled down." No structure for allowing the group to function systematically in organizational problem-solving situations was forthcoming.

In retrospect, it appears doubtful that the principal grasped how organizational training and its intended participative involvement of the staff could benefit the school program. Group process seemed to be viewed as an end, and not as a means of achieving an improved school program. Hence, the demise of meaningful professional group experiences across racial lines which were reported as having beneficial influences during and immediately after the workshop may account for some of the ground which was apparently lost in racial understandings and peer interactions toward the end of the year.

(3) One year was not a sufficient period of time for organizational training to be transferred completely into meaningful organizational development results.

Organizational development is a long-term effort. It involves planned intervention strategies intended to change the beliefs, attitudes, and values of the membership of the organization. Thus the structure of the organization is changed so that it can adapt more readily to new situations. Beckhard (1969: 15) states that it has been his experience that at least two or three years are required for meaningful organizational change to take effect and be maintained. It can readily be seen that one year was not sufficient time to achieve completely meaningful organizational development.

The stresses accompanying change are reflected in many ways as development occurs. This study has pointed out that attitudes toward leadership orientation which changed during the workshop training, changed again as a result of actual organizational practices. Frustrations were felt by staff members because of unfulfilled expectations. Periods of inactivity in problem-solving were followed by significant accomplishments. For example, long-standing problems were attacked through the development of the school policy handbook.

The year immediately following training provided sufficient time to witness some observable trends in organizational development activities. It was not, however, adequate time to assess meaningful, lasting results.

(4) The key role of the principal in the American public school and its organizational development has been reemphasized by the current study.

The trainers recognized the importance of designating someone who would have the announced responsibility of insuring that the group process approach would not be abandoned in the project school. This, logically, was felt to be the responsibility of the principal, though someone else could serve this purpose. The role of a designated internal change agent never was occupied in the project school.

Operating effectively in a school which utilizes the group problem solving, participative approach places new demands on the principal. It is doubtful if the principal of the project school recognized the necessity to change his role to become a convener of organizational problem-solving. Admittedly, two weeks of organizational training was not sufficient to provide all the necessary skills and understandings required for working collaboratively with adult professionals. It appears obvious that skills are developed through use and the key person in determining such use is the status leader—the principal.

It was illustrated in the instance of the illness of the principal that the acting principal, a fellow teacher who had participated in the workshop and who was selected by the advisory group, utilized this group fully in facing current problems. This study served to illustrate that participative organizational problem-solving cannot be expected to function adequately apart from the dynamic leadership of the principal.

## SOME REFLECTIONS

In this study, organizational training influenced the specific problems of a biracial nature occasioned by the movement toward unitary schools. Race as a factor of concern in interpersonal and professional relationships in the experimental school was significantly reduced by organizational training activities.

As previously stated, an organizational training experience of two weeks duration will not, in and of itself, insure development and maintenance of a good organizational climate. While proving to provide a positive impact upon the organization in the short run, this study supports the notion that optimum utility of organizational training will be achieved and maintained as its principles become meaningfully incorporated into the life style of the school as an organization.

There must be commitment and support from top management. If implemented at the building level, as in the case of this study, the superintendent and his staff must be knowledgeable of the organizational consequences and committed to support these. Flexibility in style for the participating organization must be accepted. If system leadership is not comfortable with the implications of full and complete utilization of the concepts of delegation and participative decision-making, caution must be raised as to the wisdom of a decision to utilize organizational training type activities for even short-range outcomes such as facilitation of the movement toward unitary schools. As documented in the case study reported in this article of a project initiated with transitory objectives uppermost in mind, the rippling effects of such learning experiences generate role and organizational expectations which have strong dysfunctional implications if not met.

The currently popular roles for the building principal as the convener of organizational problem-solving (Schmuck and Nelson, 1970) and as the school's organizational climate leader (C. G. Kettering Foundation, 1971) in retrospect were underscored by the findings of this study. Certainly the void left by the inability or unwillingness of the principal of the project school to move in this direction was most damaging. However, the unique problems of a minority group principal in a majority race school setting possibly did not receive adequate attention during the transitional stages of the desegregation process in this study. This certainly has implications for consideration as other systems move down this path.

Finally, organizational training does have great utility for use in schools or school systems in improving race relations by creating an organizational life style where problems of a racial nature or any nature are dealt with openly and freely through the ongoing processes of the organization. Certainly, as demonstrated in this study, such training experiences have very meaningful implications for the transitory processes to which educational leaders should give close attention as they move toward unitary school programs. Any decision to utilize organizational training procedures must be made, however, with the full realization that they do not lend themselves to "easy control by management in a traditional sense" once they are implemented.

## NOTE

1. "Reconstituted school" is defined as a school which has been reorganized, totally or in part, in terms of administration, faculty, nonprofessional staff, grade patterns, instructional patterns, and student bodies as a result of the desegregation process.

## REFERENCES

BECKHARD, R. (1969) Organizational Development: Strategies and Models. Reading, Mass.: Addison-Wesley.

KETTERING, C. F., C. F. Kettering Foundation (1971) "The principal as the schools climate leader: a new role for the principalship." Foundation Occasional Paper. Inglewood, Colorado.

SCHMUCK, R. A. and J. NELSON (1970) "The principal as convener of organizational problem solving." University of Colorado School of Education, Center for Field Services and Training. (mimeo)

SCHMUCK, R. A. and P. I. RUNKEL (1970) Organizational Training for a School Faculty. Eugene: Univ. of Oregon Press.

SMITH, W. S. (1965) Group Problem-Solving Through Discussion. New York: Bobbs-Merrill.